Obligations

Obligations: New Trajectories in Law provides a critical analysis of the role of obligations in contemporary legal and social practices.
  As rights have become the preeminent feature of modern political and legal discourse, the work of obligations has been overshadowed. Questioning and correcting this dominant image of our time, this book brings obligations back into view in a way that fits better with the realities of contemporary social life. Following a historical account of the changing place and priorities of obligations in modernity, the book analyses how obligations and practices of obedience are core to understanding how law sustains conditions of inequality. But it also explores the enduring role obligations play in furthering individual and collective well-being, highlighting their significance in practices that prioritize human and environmental needs, common goods, and solidarity. In doing so, it also offers an alternative and cogent assessment of the force, and the potential, of obligations in contemporary societies.
  This original jurisprudential contribution will appeal to an academic and student readership in law, politics, and the social sciences.

Scott Veitch is Paul KC Chung Professor in Jurisprudence at the University of Hong Kong.

New Trajectories in Law
Series editors
Adam Gearey, Birkbeck College, University of London
Colin Perrin, Commissioning Editor, Routledge

For information about the series and details of previous and forthcoming titles, see https://www.routledge.com/New-Trajectories-in-Law/book-series/NTL

Obligations
New Trajectories in Law

Scott Veitch

a GlassHouse Book

First published 2021
by Routledge
2 Park Square, Milton Park, Abingdon, Oxon OX14 4RN

and by Routledge
52 Vanderbilt Avenue, New York, NY 10017

A GlassHouse Book

Routledge is an imprint of the Taylor & Francis Group, an informa business

© 2021 Scott Veitch

The right of Scott Veitch to be identified as author of this work has been asserted by him in accordance with sections 77 and 78 of the Copyright, Designs and Patents Act 1988.

All rights reserved. No part of this book may be reprinted or reproduced or utilised in any form or by any electronic, mechanical, or other means, now known or hereafter invented, including photocopying and recording, or in any information storage or retrieval system, without permission in writing from the publishers.

Trademark notice: Product or corporate names may be trademarks or registered trademarks, and are used only for identification and explanation without intent to infringe.

British Library Cataloguing-in-Publication Data
A catalogue record for this book is available from the British Library

Library of Congress Cataloging-in-Publication Data
Names: Veitch, Scott, author.
Title: Obligations : new trajectories in law / Scott Veitch.
Description: Milton Park, Abingdon, Oxon ; New York, NY : Routledge, 2021. | Series: New trajectories in law | Includes bibliographical references and index.
Identifiers: LCCN 2020040501 (print) | LCCN 2020040502 (ebook) | ISBN 9780367345983 (hardback) | ISBN 9780429340796 (ebook)
Subjects: LCSH: Obligations (Law)
Classification: LCC K830 .V45 2021 (print) | LCC K830 (ebook) | DDC 346.02—dc23
LC record available at https://lccn.loc.gov/2020040501
LC ebook record available at https://lccn.loc.gov/2020040502

ISBN: 978-0-367-34598-3 (hbk)
ISBN: 978-0-429-34079-6 (ebk)

Typeset in Times New Roman
by codeMantra

Contents

Acknowledgements　vii

Introduction　1

1 **The priority of obligations: introductory observations**　8
Senses of priority 8
A note of caution 16

2 **The place of obligations: modern antecedents**　21
Divine rights and obligations 23
Donne on debt 27
Obedience, freedom, engagement 31

3 **Shifting priorities: into the modern**　36
Revolutionary rights and subterranean continuities 36
New priorities 43
A structural substitution 48

4 **The ecology of obligations: situating the legal bond**　58
Obligations in law 59
*The ecology of obligations and obligation-
　obedience hybrids 67*

5 **Hybrids in action: three contemporary legal formations**　73
Working obligations 73
Property conditions 77
Indebtedness 85

vi Contents

6 Obligations, needs, solidarities: old and new trajectories   90
Taking obligations seriously 93
Needs and obligations 98
Obligations and solidarities 102
Ecology and *obligations 110*

Bibliography   115
Index   121

Acknowledgements

My thanks to Adam Gearey and Colin Perrin for having this book in their series, and for much more besides. A number of people helped in a variety of ways and I would like to thank them all: Joxerramon Bengoetxea, Roger Cotterrell, Maks Del Mar, Grace Fung, Peter Goodrich, Valerie Kerruish, Kyle McGee, Shaun McVeigh, Lilian Moncrieff, George Pavlakos, Nigel Simmonds, Marcelo Thompson, and Johan Van Der Walt.

For comments on the manuscript in draft, and for many inspiring discussions, I am immensely grateful to Emilios Christodoulidis, Lindsay Farmer, Daniel Matthews, and Kenny Veitch. Their generosity in these and in so many other respects over the years has meant a huge amount to me, and I give them my sincere thanks. Any shortcomings in the text are none of their doing.

To my parents, and to Zach, Leon, and Corin, I am once again grateful. I have been fortunate in having them with me along the way. Ally Mackay discussed with me many of the ideas presented here. Her tolerance, compassion, and strength throughout the time it took to research and write the book have been extraordinary; she has, as ever, been an inspiration.

Finally, the memory of my grandparents has been with me in writing this. The sense of worth and wonder they saw in world are an invaluable legacy.

This book is dedicated to Ally.

SV
Hong Kong
August 2020

Introduction

We live in a world replete with obligations. Much of social life is organised through, and constituted by, the assumption, imposition, and performance of obligations. Across a broad range of social forms and institutions the binding quality of obligations is a necessary element in the social practices that hold people, groups, institutions, and activities together. And yet the work of obligations has been overshadowed by a contemporary focus on rights. As rights have become the predominant feature of political and legal discourse, in both theory and practice, it is commonly asserted that we now live in an "age of rights". This book seeks to question and correct this dominant image of our time. It brings obligations back into view in a way that fits better with the realities of contemporary social life.

It is of course true that "rights-talk" *does* have a presence that "obligations-talk" does not. We frequently refer, for example, to the importance of human rights, but speak less readily about the importance of human obligations. We bear witness to human rights violations daily in the media, though we talk much less about violations of human obligations. And it is significant that we have courts of human rights, not courts of human obligations. So even if legal rights and obligations are correlative – the idea that rights always imply a directly corresponding obligation – then our language and institutions display a prioritisation of rights that sits at odds with that idea of correlation. To describe our contemporary legal and political culture as equally an "age of obligations" seems not only strange, but contrary to the spirit of the times.

Mainstream as well as critical legal theorists have tended to endorse this asymmetry and prioritisation by concentrating overly on the work rights do. This book shifts perspective by focusing on the work obligations do, and considers how and why this work is obscured. To do so it is necessary to examine a range of factors in the social, economic, and

2   *Introduction*

cultural contexts within which rights and obligations currently operate, and to highlight the specific ways in which obligations do their work, ways that tend not to be discussed in current legal theory.

One of the tasks of this book then is to draw attention to the ways in which obligations appear, and disappear, in contemporary discourses. To understand how and why this occurs requires tracing where and how obligations work, and what practical and conceptual conditions they draw on and facilitate. And in particular it requires understanding how they relate to social practices of obedience by examining what are identified here as obligation-obedience hybrids. It is in comprehending these conditions and practices that we can understand better our legal culture and its dominant values and patterns of behaviour in ways that "right-talk" and even "rights critique" do not.

This book is mainly descriptive. Apart from the final chapter in which the potential of obligations is examined through the lens of solidarity, it seeks to describe, or perhaps re-describe, familiar aspects of contemporary law and society, albeit, hopefully, in an original manner. One implication of this is worth stating clearly: in its focus on obligations this book is not making an argument, as some critical accounts might, that rights are incompatible with certain kinds of social and political progress. The beliefs, writings, and actions of activists and dissidents who have fought – and in many countries are still fighting – against violations of human dignity, discrimination, and exploitation by state and non-state actors provide ample support for the observation that "a rejection of rights discourse can only be promoted by relatively privileged people who take their rights for granted" (Davies 2017, p. 5; see also Williams 1987). Taking more account of obligations does not entail devaluing rights as such. That said, two points should be noted. First, some of the most important effects of certain kinds of rights, especially those associated with dominant practices and interpretations of private law doctrines of property and contract, are such that they structure possibilities of action and thinking so profoundly that they appear as mere common sense. But they are also – clearly – neither equally beneficial to all nor could they be in their present form. With respect to property law for instance, citizens' freedom of movement within a jurisdiction may be curtailed by the constitution, distribution, and legal enforcement of private rights in land; in this way people's homes and individual property are protected from interference. But when a broader perspective on this is taken the effects look different. A recent survey, for example, found that even today "around a third of England and Wales remains in the hands of the aristocracy and landed gentry – and half of England is owned by less than 1 per cent of the population" (Shrubsole 2019, p. 88). As a consequence, "just 10 per cent of England and Wales is open-access land; 90 percent remains off-limits to the public" (ibid., p. 252). The protection, under the rule of law, of private property rights in land thus immunises social and political relations from efforts at progressive change that would seek to, and would need to, disturb these patterns and assumptions if a more egalitarian society was to be established. In addition to this, there is a tendency to think that questions of distribution are predominantly matters of *re*distribution through public policies such as taxation. But the more profound forms of distribution have often already been embedded *before* these take place, in the private law doctrines that create and protect inequalities of distributions in the name of the law. But as RH Tawney observed, "If the rules of a game give permanent advantage to some of the players, it does not become fair merely because they are scrupulously observed by all who take part in it" (Tawney 1964, p. 116). Rights matter then, but in ways that need to be sensitive to their context and functioning: to what and who they protect, and what and who they make vulnerable.

Second, rights are deeply reliant on obligations since obligations and practices of obedience structure the operation and effectiveness of rights themselves. With some exceptions, this has been largely neglected in legal analysis. Where it is taken notice of it is usually with the aim of understanding how to make rights more effective (Waldron 1989). But if, as we have just noted, making rights effective may produce and sustain widespread patterns of inequality, then more critical attention to the labours of obligation is required. To do so is not to offer more criticisms of rights, but something that approaches the problems differently, something that might be called an obligations critique.

Such observations form the general background for this book. They suggest that obligations – and how and why they operate as they do – deserve more attention than they have hitherto received in jurisprudential scholarship. This book therefore details the ways in which obligations work, assesses their assumptions and effects, and provides an opportunity to re-think their position, and their potential, in social, political, and legal practices.

Given that this is the aim of the book, let me briefly say something about how the approach taken here relates to what is conventionally known as the law of obligations. The latter is traditionally understood as one of the two pillars of private law, the other being the law of property. The law of obligations deals with personal rights, whilst property law deals with "real" rights and the difference between the two, as explained by Peter Birks, arises from the question: "From whom can rights be demanded?" The law of obligations concerns those rights that are "exigible [i.e. demandable] only against the person against whom they first arise or that person's representatives" (Birks 2000, p. xxxviii). "Real rights", by contrast, "can be demanded from any person in whose hands the thing is found" (ibid). Drawing on a taxonomy that reaches back to the Roman lawyer Gaius in the second century AD, personal rights can be further subdivided by asking another question: "From what events do rights arise?" (ibid, p. xxxix). And the answers to this question divide around the presence or lack of consent. This produces a schema familiar to all law students: contracts, which arise from consent, and torts (or delicts), unjust enrichment, and what Birks calls "miscellaneous other events" (ibid., xlii), which do not. In broad terms, then, personal rights arise from either voluntary or non-voluntary events and the right in both cases "is a right to some kind of performance from the person under the obligation" (ibid., p. xl). In this way is the "law of obligations", as correlative personal rights and obligations, conventionally understood and taught, and it is perhaps no more than a quirk that this category of rights "has always been identified from the negative end and called, not 'duties', but 'obligations'" (ibid., p. xxxix).

This book does not engage directly with this taxonomy nor does it seek to challenge it. Instead, it takes a broader view of obligations in law. According to Charles Fried, "Law speaks the language of obligation" (Fried 2015, p. 1), but it does so in many registers and not only with respect to the "law of obligations". Thus obligations are a key component of the way law governs many different aspects of social regulation (and social life), including criminal law, the law of taxation, public, administrative, and welfare law, company law, and so on. Across all these areas of legal activity we find the presence of obligations in seeking to guide, constrain, and facilitate the behaviour of legal actors. Indeed, the definition of an obligation in Roman private law is sufficiently broad to enable us to see how it can be found in all these varied legal settings. As expressed in Justinian's *Institutes*, "An obligation is a bond of law, by which we are tied down to the necessity of making some performance, according to the laws of the state" (Birks 2014, p. 2). Understood in these terms – terms to which we will return later in the book – it can already be seen that obligations form a core component not only of the law of contracts and torts, but of private law generally, as well as public and criminal law too. So the reason for taking a wider view of obligations in law is that limiting ourselves to the conventional law of obligations would miss too much about how obligations work and the role they play. While reference will be made in places to the traditional domain of the law of obligations, it is to this more extensive range that the book refers.

Given this, let me also say a brief word about the selection of material I have used here to analyse the role of obligations, for this too is wide-ranging. In a line to which we will return, the celebrated English jurist HLA Hart observed that "[t]he figure of a bond binding the person obligated, which is buried in the word 'obligation', and the similar notion of a debt latent in the word 'duty' ... haunts much legal thought" (Hart 1961, p. 85). In part, this book is a sustained reflection on that "haunting" as it seeks to trace lineages and contemporary presences (and absences) of this spectral figure. But despite Hart's provocation, this "figure" has remained remarkably under-examined in jurisprudential writings. Certainly, much of the legal philosophy that followed in Hart's wake has tended to ignore or downplay the range of symbolic and material forces that law works with to "bind the person obligated". Instead, the interest in obligations has been taken up as a matter of addressing reasons for action that an individual might have in weighing up what to do. In doing this it assumes a rather anaemic, stick-figure picture of people and their surroundings, one in which individual citizens have little more to do than carry out moral and legal calculations about the reasons they have to act in relation to other such figures. There is little of the flesh-and-blood of real lives: of family and work conditions, property and rental markets, personal dynamics of debt, insecurity, or illness – all these relationships and experiences and challenges that make contemporary lives what they are. Nor is there an integration into these analyses of the power of the institutions that are central and ineliminable features of everyday life – bureaucracies, banks, corporations, administrative agencies, and the like. These contexts and conditions within which people's lives are led and their opportunities opened or closed all seem strangely, if not perversely, absent from much of legal philosophy. This inevitably makes it of limited value if we are interested in how law works in society. It is rather like seeking a description of a great ocean liner and being told only about the choices available on the menu in the first-class dining room. "Yes, but how does this ship *move*?" we would want to know. To offer a richer and more dynamic sense of the work of legal practices and concepts, specifically here with regard to obligations, effort needs to be made to take into account a more diverse range of social, political, and historical material. And to do this, not only legal literature but other forms of scholarship and reflection are necessary and, one hopes, insightful.

This has one final implication. This book appears in a series called "New Trajectories in Law". Yet, in order to provide something "new" in this setting it seems to me essential to reach into the past to do so. Trajectories have, one might imagine, a historical arc, and so an awareness of the contingencies and opportunities of the present requires a certain tracing or even reimagining of that arc. For this reason, Chapters 2 and 3 reach back to offer an account of the trajectory of obligations that can inform their present situation. This does not provide a history of obligations as such, a project that would require much more space than is available here. Instead, it observes a transitional shift according to which rights discourses come to the fore as obligations recede from dominant theoretical and political accounts. But this transition conceals a continuity in the work required of obligations, a continuity that is registered in the uneven and unequal realities of present social practices and experiences. Obligations, one might say, go subterranean. But in doing so they continue to provide the basis of social and legal developments nonetheless.

To offer a "new trajectory" therefore requires excavating aspects of this process and in doing so it also sheds new light on the idea of modernity ushering in an age of rights. Central to this is the *place* of obligations in the schemas of thought that frame social practices and expectations. The argument made in Chapter 3 is that the priority of obligations does not disappear as societies move away from the dominance of religious belief to secular societies proclaiming the rights of man. Rather, a structural substitution occurs in which religious dogma is replaced by other forms that are similarly, if less apparently, marked by the continuity of the priority of obligations. The central structural form of substitution is from religion to economy, but it is complemented by other forms of obligation and practices of obedience, including those attuned to maintaining the imposed asymmetries specific to race and gender. So it is in this sense that a "new trajectory" must start from where the "old" one finds itself. But that, I argue here, is not where it might be expected.

This insight is developed in Chapter 4, which examines what is termed here the ecology of obligations. The ecological aspect refers to the ways in which obligations are relationally and reflexively situated within wider social structures. In this setting hybrids of obligation and obedience underpin and facilitate the circulation of legal obligations throughout social practices in ways that are not adequately foregrounded by a focus on rights. So while legal obligations as legal bonds do specific work, the features of which are set out at the start of Chapter 4, it is their relation to broader practices of obedience and conformity that explain more adequately their operation in modern society. But as the examples taken up in Chapter 5 – examples that refer to work, property, and debt – show, these forms are also central today in maintaining conditions whereby inequality and unequal opportunities continue to be dominant.

The final chapter addresses the positive work that obligations do in maintaining communal and individual flourishing. For if obligations provide ways of constraining and disciplining people, they also have the capacity to secure relationships of trust and solidarity. This requires paying attention not only to collective action, organisation, and resources, but to the more foundational problematic of our common dependencies and vulnerabilities. Chapter 6 argues that while rights rely for their protection on the operation of multiple obligations, it is a deeper sense of obligation, one grounded in individual and collective needs, that offers a better way of understanding the potential that obligations have in sustaining communal well-being. The chapter thus ends by contending that this potential must be directed towards critiquing the limitations of certain dominant conceptions of rights, in particular those that legitimate the production, distribution, and consumption practices which threaten animal and plant life on our planet. The deep reliance humans and other species have on ecological conditions suggests turning our attention back to the priority of obligations in order to provide a way of reimagining our relationships with the natural world.

Obligations cannot, of course, solve all such problems. But thinking about their modes of operation in contemporary society, and their complex potential in forms of solidarity, may set readers off on a new trajectory, one that challenges the dominant self-image of our time.

1 The priority of obligations
Introductory observations

Senses of priority

For most of known human history there were no such things as rights. They were creations of the Western imagination some time in the first half of the second millennium AD. They gained widespread credibility slowly and achieved predominance, and even then unevenly, with the advent of modernity and the rise of capitalism. The same cannot be said of obligations. The metaphorical "tying" of people together which lies at the core of the idea and practice of obligation has been a constant in human societies. These bonds and ties – of people to each other and to things: ideas, gods, God, nature, the earth, institutions, the past, the future, the dead, the not-yet born – form core connective elements in the organisation and imaginaries of all societies. Through enormous social, economic, and technological changes, obligations of kinship, reciprocity, and belonging have, amongst others, provided means for binding communities together over long stretches of time and distance. The pervasiveness and resilience of obligations have thus been central to communities' maintenance and reproduction in a way that rights have not. The idea that rights and obligations are correlative is therefore a highly contingent and modern one.

In this section we will consider several different senses of the priority of obligations first by briefly introducing some historical and comparative examples, before turning in more detail to consider how linguistic communication embodies ethical and symbolic dimensions that continue to operate through priorities of obligation. The intention is not to be comprehensive, but merely to show how obligations historically, and in many respects still today, have a primacy in social institutions and relations.

One of the most striking examples of the priority of obligations in social and political thought may be found in China, "by far and away the oldest continuously existing polity in the world" (Jacques 2012, p. 244). Ancient Chinese thought and civilisation formed the basis for a highly sophisticated, if strictly hierarchical, tradition that was sustained for more than two millennia across a vast territory and population. In its dominant Confucian form there were personal and official virtues to be learned and practised, vices to be avoided, and strict rules setting out obligatory norms of correct conduct at different levels of family and administrative hierarchies (Chang 2016). Morality was cultivated and culture transmitted through the practice of rites, roles, and offices. But "[t]he concept of the rights of the individual or the people did not exist. The traditional legal system was based on people's duties and obligations rather than their rights and interests" (Chen 2004, p. 17). For longer still, First Nation peoples of Australia (and elsewhere) had successfully sustained relationships with each other and the land through practising a living law that understood human societies as part of a continuum with nature. Knowledge and responsibilities were passed down from ancestors and elders to succeeding generations through songs and stories which formed "a natural system of obligations and benefits, flowing from an Aboriginal ontology" (Watson 2014, p. 5). The range of ties – spatial, temporal, and conceptual – existed within a cosmology which emphasised care for relationships among people and their environment: "Indigenous knowledges, unlike those of Europe, carry obligations and responsibilities, such as custodial obligations to ruwe [land] that bind future generations" (ibid., p. 14). The transmission of intergenerational experience and obligations in these forms was thus alien to any idea of rights as individual or collective claims to property in or sovereignty over land. As with many other societies colonised by Europeans in the modern era, when rights did come – in the ships, minds, and doctrines of the colonisers – they would quickly be deployed as part of the intellectual weaponry that, along with the cannons and guns, would justify theft and the devastation of a way of life and law that had endured for tens of thousands of years.

Great religions too have prioritised obligations without a sense of rights. Robert Cover noted just how central obligation and practices of obedience have been to Jewish life and culture: "The basic word of Judaism is 'obligation' or *mitzvah*". Obligations, Cover argued, not only had a preeminence, but Judaism treated the modes of entitlement that rights might describe as out of place in defining well-being. Instead, "to be one who acts out of obligation is the closest thing there is to a Jewish definition of completion as a person within the community"

10 The priority of obligations

(Cover 1987, pp. 66–67). Buddhism likewise prioritised the notion of reciprocal obligation and has no term for rights. And one looks in vain in the Christian bible for precepts that begin "It is your right to ..." Rather, it was only by internalising and observing the obligations and guidance of Christ's teachings that the faithful might find the spiritual path to living good lives. Alasdair MacIntyre sums up these brief observations well:

> [T]here is no expression in any ancient or medieval language correctly translated by our expression 'a right' until near the close of the middle ages: the concept lacks any means of expression in Hebrew, Greek, Latin or Arabic, classical or medieval, before about 1400, let alone in Old English, or in Japanese even as late as the mid-nineteenth century.
>
> (MacIntyre 1985, p. 69)

Historically then, there is no doubt that sophisticated legal, political, and economic orders could and did operate without any conception of rights, and that they could and did do so with extensive geographical and temporal reach and success. This was also importantly true of the lengthy formative period of the Western legal tradition itself, namely, with respect to Roman Law. "The classical Romans", noted Richard Tuck, "did not have a theory about legal relationships in which the modern notion of a subjective right played any part" (Tuck 1978, p. 12). Yet they developed elaborate procedural, adjudicative, and enforcement mechanisms which were central to carrying out, among other things, complex economic activities. This comprised a conceptually innovative system of private law which allowed for the creation and enforcement of debtors' obligations to creditors. But here too there was no conception of rights:

> [T]he Roman texts do not speak in terms of rights, but only in terms of various performances enforceable by creditors ... the focus, from the creditor's perspective, is on whichever *actio* might be available to him for the redress of the debtor's failure to perform. What is crucial is having an action ... not the abstract concept of a 'right'.
>
> (Hogg 2017, pp. 19, 29)

Throughout its early and classical periods, and even after Justinian's restatement of Roman Law in the sixth century AD, a complex legal system operated which was replete with actions and obligations, but with nothing that would be recognisable to the moderns as rights.

It was only 500 years later, when the Roman Law texts were rediscovered and studied by scholars in the early European universities, that "the personal link created through an obligational relationship came to be analysed as giving rise to a *ius in personam* (a personal right) on the creditor's part" (ibid., p. 29).

In these ancient, institutional, and non-Western examples we can clearly identify the priority obligations have had historically. There are other manifestations of this priority that continue even in contemporary societies in which rights have come to play an important role. We owe to obligations, in fact, much of the textured ordering of our daily lives. Language use is the most obvious example. By learning the rules of a language we come to understand and to communicate in ways that are necessarily dependent upon others and which, in time, come to offer the opportunity for self-expression. Our potential for autonomous thought or communication is therefore reliant on being able to learn to follow obligatory rules that initially define what and how things can be said correctly and then, potentially, allow us to create new meanings for ourselves and others. "What we call 'society'", writes Alain Supiot, "is a weave of speech binding people together", in which obligations exist through the "words and texts that bind me to others" (Supiot 2007, pp. viii–ix). The reliance of individuals on collective structures of language has an inescapable quality which is at the same time potentially liberating:

> If we are to enjoy thinking and expressing ourselves freely in a language, we must first submit to the limits that give words meaning; without this radical heteronomy, we would have no autonomy ... That is, before we can dispose of ourselves freely and say "I", we are already a subject of law, bound – *sub-jectum*: thrown under – by words which ties us to others.
>
> (ibid., p. viii)

In a theme to which we will return, binding ties supplied by obligations may be at once constraining and potentially liberating. And so we should understand that language use also carries something of profound significance that goes beyond the mere *content* of what is being communicated. Neil MacCormick explained this well:

> The power of speech is one of the irreducibly social powers of the human mind. The conditions of learning and using speech depend absolutely on a common adherence to the common norms of grammar and the like that structure our speech.
>
> (MacCormick 2008, p. 28)

But such structures of speech, he added, include not only the "common norms" found in these grammatical rules (how to conjugate verbs or use tenses correctly and so on) but also rules that have a *moral* character. Such rules are usually implicit but are absolutely vital to the working of language as a means of communication. As MacCormick put it, these common norms "must include a norm favouring truthfulness and sincerity over falsehood and cheating, for a community without such norms would either never develop a language or swiftly lose the one they have" (ibid.). The "highly normative" quality of language thus involves users learning *additional* standards of right and wrong which they are obligated to respect – such as those of truthfulness and sincerity – if they are to be able to use the language properly or even at all. What is significant about this, concludes MacCormick, is that all this occurs

> without any human act of will clad with some form of institutional authority ... The moral is that we humans are norm-users first before we are norm-creators, or legislators. If so, it follows that *our sense of duty and obligation to each other is and has to be prior* to any authoritative imposition of rules upon us. Were it not so, civil institutions could never have developed
>
> (ibid., p. 29, emphasis added)

Such communal, linguistic, and moral obligations thus furnish another key sense of the priority of obligations, one on which positive laws and institutions are themselves reliant. If, as we noted in the Introduction, "[l]aw speaks the language of obligation" (Fried 2015), in order to do so it must draw accordingly *on* that language and the set of expectations and dispositions that already exist within it.

That language has this deep moral aspect does not mean, of course, that it may not be used for perfectly immoral purposes: to wound, to humiliate, to cheat and lie. But these too rely on the ability of speech to communicate meaning successfully; there is even in these cases an implicit obligation to make intelligible such damaging assertions. To lie intentionally, for example, requires some ability and obligation (on the speaker) to discriminate between what is true and what is false even to communicate the latter; and to be deceived (as a listener) also means that effective (if deceitful) communication has been achieved. (It has been said that this is why President Trump isn't really lying when he changes his story so often about what he thinks or what he has previously said: to lie means to know the *difference* between truth and falsehood and it is precisely *this* that he lacks.)

The moral quality in the nature of ordinary language use finds its place then in the connections or bonds between speakers established through the medium of language. Obligations in language establish reciprocal ties among speakers and listeners and in so doing carry the potential for achieving not only communication and institutional forms, but an elemental form of *trust* among them. Some scholars, such as Jurgen Habermas, have built complex theories of ethics, politics, and law up from these capacities of "communicative rationality" and the obligatory conditions they entail and supply. Indeed, Habermas argues there is an increasing centrality to reliance on these functions of language in the modern world. As societies have become more secular, he argues, sacred beliefs are no longer persuasive reference points of credibility or validity and instead language itself and its shared structures become key. "Convictions owe their authority less and less to the spellbinding power and the aura of the holy, and more and more to a consensus that is not merely reproduced but *achieved*, that is, brought about communicatively" (Habermas 1987, p. 89, emphasis in original). And this achievement is realised, Habermas adds, through the "binding effect of consensus formation in language" (ibid.). Much of the time these conditions are so deeply implicit that their success in binding together speakers and listeners is such that we take them for granted. With the "linguistification of the sacred" (to use Habermas's unlovely term) these conditions may no longer be *spell* binding; but they are binding nonetheless.

Yet even now these conditions are sometimes formalised and made perspicuous, binding the speaker explicitly through linguistic or other symbolic or material means (Constable 2014). This may happen with respect to truth-claims set against different temporal horizons, as when, for example, a witness about to make statements about some past event in court will be asked to "solemnly swear" to tell the truth before giving evidence. While the purely symbolic forms of this may be in relative decline we still find them in a variety of settings, such as the oaths required in the swearing-in ceremonies of legislators, judges, and other officials – raising the hand, placing it on a book, and so on – or in legal rituals that retain a direct religious dimension, such as can be found in some marriage ceremonies. Likewise, with respect to the present and future, evidential formalities commonly rely on subscribing an individual's signature to mark that the promise to perform a particular act at some future point is intended to have legal consequences. Obligations used daily in spoken language are thus often given an additional "guarantee" to assure and confirm their binding quality. In many of these ritualised formalities – which typically need to take place before an audience – the speaker is asked to acknowledge an external guarantor for the obligations they are assuming. This might take different forms: their God, the monarch, the People, or the Party. It is an old question as to whether this adds a second obligation, or merely just an additional strengthening to the original obligation. According to Pufendorf, it is the latter: "[O]aths do not of themselves produce a new and peculiar obligation, but are only applied as an additional bond to the obligation in its nature valid before" (quoted in Agamben 2011, p. 5). And when that doubly strengthened bond is broken by the speaker, there may be, as there still is today, serious consequences.

In all these contexts such obligations supply something else of great importance: they also bring about an obligation on the *hearer* to accept the quality of what has been said. As Kerrigan writes of the use of "binding language" in practices such as oath-taking: "You are bound to what you say, but also bound to those whose acceptance of your word might be thought to leave *them* with an obligation to trust that meshes with your responsibility to speak the truth" (Kerrigan 2016, p. 10, emphasis added). In a formal way, this is an exemplification of the deeper structuring of the mutuality of relations made possible by the reciprocal assumption of obligations through language.

Beyond these linguistic aspects, obligations exhibit a priority within certain practices that form part of the ineliminable makeup of social life. Perhaps most intensely, family, intimate relations, and friendships are all practices that rely on a more or less dense network of obligations. Their regular or appropriate fulfilment allows us to rely on others, and to make ourselves reliable. Thus, like language they form an essential aspect in establishing and sustaining trust within relationships. Of course, there are other features in these relationships, besides obligations: affection, desire, loyalty, love, tolerance, compassion, and the like. And, of course, too, not all obligations that grow out of these relationships are all the time welcomed. But at core they are, and for one key reason: although obligations constrain, in doing so they are not necessarily, and sometimes not at all, irksome. As Harry Frankfurt observed analogously about one of these contexts: "It is partly just because loving does bind our wills that we value it as we do … the necessities with which love binds the will are themselves liberating [and are experienced as] an expansion of ourselves" (Frankfurt 2000, p. 15). Obligations arise as part of what it means to be in and to value particular relationships in themselves: being bound in these ways contributes to our growth, our sense of being and being together with

The priority of obligations 15

others in the world. Obligations are central to this because they work by connecting, by tying us to others. "The origins of normativity", writes Frankfurt, "lie in the contingent necessities of love", and the welcome fulfilment of obligations – what he calls those *"irresistible requirements"* of love – thus form part of the dispositions, actions, and affects that are constitutive of these relationships as they – and we, if we are fortunate – develop over time (ibid., p. 7, emphasis added).

To think that the obligations of love – or of friendship, or other such relations – are purely the result of an individual's reasoned choices is as mistaken as thinking they could be purchased with money. This would fail to understand, or experience, what these relationship are. In the complex weave of social lives in which these obligations are essential, individual rational choice and utility maximisation have no place, and we would doubt the capacity for love or friendship in someone who thought they did.

It is striking then that while obligations do not seem out of place in such relationships – indeed, as we have just seen, they appear as central to them – rights certainly do. Unlike obligations, rights can do no connective work here. For someone to assert they have a right to love or to friendship seems not only misguided but desperate. Perhaps it was for this reason that Thomas Jefferson did not carelessly throw in the idea of a "right to happiness" on the list of inalienable rights he set out in the American Declaration of Independence. What was inalienable, he said, was only the right to pursue it. And this right, and this freedom, if it ended with successfully achieving happiness in relations of love and friendship, would be experienced through being part of a web of obligations – those irresistible requirements – that would simultaneously constrain behaviour and enhance well-being.

In a related sense, but with respect to a different and broader-ranging set of practices, obligations also form a primary element in the wider networks of transmission and exchange essential to the reproduction of social relations even amongst strangers. Here obligations play a key role in facilitating certain exchanges. But they also have an important role in *preventing* certain other kinds of exchange. That is, they can operate to protect the integrity of practices from the corrosive effects of commensuration to other logics, such as monetary value. The significance of this was highlighted by the anthropologist Maurice Godelier. All societies, he writes, rely on the exchange of things. Exchange occurs either through acts that detach things from their original holder (such as in selling something to someone by way of contractual agreement) or by transferring them in such a way that something of their presence continues to exist in the relation (as in the case of gifts). In this latter form

> things are both detached from their owner since this person has given them up, but remain attached to him or her, since they have been given and the giver remains present in the thing that has been given, thereby creating obligations to the giver.
> (Godelier 2011, p. 419)

But there is a further aspect to this which is, says Godelier, true with respect to all exchanges and signifies the foundational role of obligations. Thus, he continues, "in order for some things to circulate, others must remain *stationary* and serve as anchor points for the basic components of the society's organization and thereby the identity of the individual and group members" (ibid., emphasis in original). These things take on an *inalienable* quality: while they can and should be *transmitted* to future generations, they cannot be exchanged for something else if they are to do their work. In societies where religion is prominent these might include, for example, sacred objects or places. In secular societies they might be such things as a constitution or "justice" or "due process". These cannot be commodified but instead they provide the "stationary" basis for other kinds of exchange to take place. Indeed, attempts to buy or sell them would transform them into something else – their opposite in fact: corruption.

Gathering together these observations Godelier concludes that societies rest on two principles:

> [T]he obligation to give and the obligation not to give what must be kept in order to transmit it ... The life of societies, like that of the individuals that compose them, thus rests on two distinct but complementary and necessary obligations: the obligation to exchange and the obligation to keep and transmit.
> (ibid., pp. 429, 470)

Maintaining the integrity of the stationary points is thus both communal and obligatory. It is in this sense too that obligations continue to play a foundational, structuring, and constitutive role in communities, a role that has not been superseded even in our "age of rights".

A note of caution

We have seen how, in addition to historical and cultural examples mentioned earlier, the existence and use of obligations in language and in

The priority of obligations 17

elementary if complex forms of social relations gives obligations a priority and centrality in sustaining these relations. Yet the idea that there are, in Godelier's phrase, "necessary obligations" has, nonetheless, been insufficiently recognised in many contemporary jurisprudential analyses. One of the challenges in correcting this lies, however, in understanding that (and how) the work done by obligations varies with the settings in which they operate. This has two related dimensions. On the one hand, what counts as "necessary" may vary over time and place and that variation may be the result of some power struggle to institute it *as* necessary. On the other hand, what may be seen as a positively valuable role of obligations in one context may be negative in others. For example, the priority of obligations of friendships or family that are positive features of social life may be out of place if they appear in contexts that transform their meaning to a negative one. In the setting of public office, for example, acting on familial obligations may be seen as straightforwardly nepotistic and harmful to the equal opportunities of others. The potentially positive and negative effects of obligations will thus be context sensitive. To borrow a formulation from Stanley Milgram's famous experiments on obedience to authority, a "calculated restructuring of the informational and social field" (Milgram 1974, p. 7) can transform the meaning and purpose of obligations. It will be the focus of Chapter 5 to explore in detail the ways in which the contemporary contexts and practices within which obligations are deployed may be profoundly negative from the perspective of other standpoints and values. But for the moment, we should strike a note of caution with respect to the matter of their priority.

That this may be true in a more general sense can be seen through considering certain historically significant instances. For example, if Roman Law had, as we have seen, no concept of rights but a highly developed account and practice of obligations, this is not in itself a ground to praise it unequivocally or even at all. For Roman Law also had a highly developed account and practice of slavery. And on one view the two may not be entirely dissociable. William Galbraith Miller in his remarkable and largely forgotten book, *The Data of Jurisprudence*, argued that "[s]lavery is the starting point of obligation. In this institution we find the physical meeting point of the ideas of property, obligation, and political subjection" (Miller 1903, p. 139). Miller was a contemporary of Nietzsche, who had also (and more famously) asserted that moral obligations had their origins in the physical, coercive methods of Roman Law. For Nietzsche, moral obligations did not provide the foundations for legal institutions. It was the other way round: the force of moral obligations was grounded in the legal concept of debt which, as it had developed in the early Roman Law of the Twelve

Tables, authorised creditors to inflict *physical* damage on debtors in cases of default. In Nietzsche's view, "It is in *this* sphere, in legal obligation, then that the moral conceptual world of 'guilt', 'conscience', 'duty', 'sacred duty' originates – its beginning, like the beginning of everything great on earth, has long been steeped in blood" (Nietzsche 1996, p. 46, emphasis in original). With respect to obligations then, Zimmermann notes that the

> very word 'obligatio' always reminded the Roman lawyer of the fact that, in former times, the person who was to be liable, that is over whose body the creditor acquired the pledge-like power of seizure, was physically laid in bonds.
>
> (Zimmermann 1996, p. 5)

That the debtor "ought to", or as we still say "was bound to", do whatever was legally required of him therefore had its antecedents in the fact that he was *literally* "bound" to do it.

The origins of *concepts* such as obligation were thus, on these accounts, to be found in the *material* infliction of suffering. In this respect, says Miller, the concept of obligation is "typical of leading legal ideas, [in which] we shall find a physical foundation, a gradual idealising, and in many cases finally a new physical application" (Miller 1903, p. 33). It was from such physical, coercive acts that the force of obligations derived: pain, Nietzsche observed, was a great teacher in getting people to "see reason" and to remember to keep their promises. And this could be contrasted with the creditor's experience of the relationship, something both he and Miller saw as celebratory in the infliction of cruelty. As Miller put it, "The notion of obligation or duty seems to carry with it pain or suffering – passivity – and hereby it is distinguished from the pleasurable activity of right" (ibid., p. 135). (Which could explain why the British colloquially refer to prisoners being held "at Her Majesty's pleasure".)

How much credence we can give to this account of the genesis of morality need not worry us here (compare Graeber 2012, pp. 76ff). What does matter is the recognition that one of the most significant features of obligations is that they may be both a source and an expression of valuable attachment and – as the example of the Roman Law of slavery makes particularly clear – a means of subjection and harsh treatment. To expose and understand the fact of their priority must not therefore entail necessarily valorising it: context matters. So, for example, when Honore argued that there was a fundamental or "basic norm of society" which "prescribes that the members of the society have a duty to co-operate with one another" (Honore 1987, p. 111), he drew attention to the kind of social and moral obligations and interdependencies of the kind we outlined in the previous section. But when he traces the source of this norm to a postulated commonality – "It is common enterprise ... that turns out in the end to constitute the seed of group membership and so of social obligation" (ibid., p. 63) – we need to be wary. It is true, as we have seen, that obligations are fundamental to desirable practices of co-operation and co-ordination that have a priority as features of any society. But there is a world of difference between the existence of such norms and claiming that society can or should be understood as a common enterprise. For at the level of society generally, "common enterprise" is far more rare than Honore's claim seems to suggest. Indeed, where that society and its "enterprises" are capitalist – never mind one involving slavery – its members are far from being engaged "in common" with each other where some members rely for their benefits on the exploitation of others. Obligations in such instances are central to maintaining the *lack* of commonality that is the fate of those whose labour is exploited for others' profit.

In this sense the strategic deployment of obligations for *uncommon* ends may be far more prevalent both historically and today than is their emanation and embodiment in genuinely co-operative activities. The important cautionary implication is therefore that in addressing the role and priority of obligations, we need to be attentive to their asymmetric distribution.

I will return to aspects of these observations later. But in the next two chapters I want to suggest that the priority of obligation has had a profound but shifting appearance and influence in Western legal thinking and practice. To see how, I will briefly outline two different forms that have been influential in the modern era. To organise a potentially vast amount of material I will consider, first, obligation's priority in the combination of religious and political power in the early modern period, and how this was central to the constitution of individual subjectivity. Second, I will consider the position that obligations took in the emerging discourse of rights as exemplified in works of the late seventeenth and eighteenth centuries. The analysis here will focus on how obligations' apparent *de*-prioritisation in the rights-based, social contract thinking so influential in the revolutions that ushered in the modern era masked their continuing, if displaced, priority. Obligations, in other words, continued to play a decisive role in the constitution of identities, but in altered form, and their role within political and social practices and opportunities likewise continued but mutated. Their functioning went, so to speak, underground. Or at least it did so, as we will see, from the *dominant* legal perspective and its propagators. For others – many others – there was nothing masked or hidden about the operation of obligations.

I should note two things about the brief historical account that follows. First, it is beyond the scope of this book to provide a detailed history of the changing nature of obligation's role. Rather, the aim is to establish the modes of obligation's presence that continue to find resonances in contemporary societies, for it is these that form the main focus of the later chapters of the book. It is not of course the case that the historical writers we will consider foresaw something with which we have since become familiar; it is rather that what they wrote about and conceptualised, and what was influential about these, have not been sufficiently emphasised from the contemporary perspective of obligations. And it is this – as well as certain continuities – that make them worthy of fresh consideration. Second, this short account will not do justice to the full range of cultural, religious, and institutional manifestations of the priority of obligations and their development. If I concentrate on certain aspects of Western and Christian thinking here it is not because the others lack significance but because, unlike other state or civilisational forms (such as China) and religions (such as Judaism), they also played an explicitly legitimating role in sustaining unequal, hierarchical societies and colonial expropriations that had global, and enduring, consequences.

2 The place of obligations
Modern antecedents

If any historical period can lay claim to being self-consciously an age of obligations then the seventeenth century has to be a leading contender. The networks of personal bonds and allegiances that had held together the feudal structure of landholding and military organisation which patterned Europe for centuries had not yet been entirely superseded. Below the lordly level of the old feudal law, much of society remained bound within customary, canon, and local laws in which rights had little or no developed or consistent presence. The apparatus and methods of the state had, however, been gaining momentum, becoming increasingly centralised, vigilant, and jurisdictionally jealous and thus more directly demanding of people's loyalties. Most significant of all, the power, prevalence, and deeply engrained role of religious belief and observance in everyday life existed in a way that is now difficult to imagine. We might get some sense of it by observing religious states today in which there are parallels in terms of religion's political and personal presence and potency; the use of religious courts to police and sanction people's behaviour and thought; and the routine public denigration of women (which had in the West included widespread killings on charges of witchcraft well into the seventeenth century). In the post-Reformation climate, clashes over religious doctrine and dogma, rituals and symbols, conscience and toleration resulted in obligations of obedience being tightly formulated and strictly imposed. The loyalties of subjects and officials were constantly tested through oaths of allegiance, renewed religious covenants and the like, and the consequences for non-conformity were always potentially severe. With the King at the apex of the earthly hierarchy, ties of faith and fealty thus combined to secure complex relations of governance among the multiple legal forms that crisscrossed territories. In these conditions, an "ideology of obedience" (Kerrigan 2016, p. 375) prevailed and its effects were real, pervasive, and deeply felt.

Yet rights *were* becoming more central in the political imaginary in part due to developments in natural law thinking within the Christian tradition. This was true both as a matter of conceptual analysis and in the ways in which political and social ordering was being organised. A complex series of transmissions, translations, and evolutions make it impossible to pinpoint exactly when the concept of rights emerged, and scholars disagree. Michel Villey traces their origins to the fourteenth century, some seek them earlier, others look to the sixteenth century (whilst Minogue suggests that the idea of *human* rights is "as modern as the internal combustion engine"; quoted in Tierney 2001, p. 3; Moyn 2010 dates their salience far more recently than this). Central to the longstanding older tradition was the term "ius" (derived from Roman and natural law sources) but its meaning and signification had changed over time. For Villey, "ius" originally meant "something objective, 'that which is right' in a particular situation" (Tuck 1978, p. 8). As Tierney puts it, "When Aristotle or Aquinas sought to define *dikaion* or *ius*, they did not proclaim the rights and powers of individuals. They were concerned rather with a harmonious structure of relationships, right proportion, *just partage*" (Tierney 2001, p. 22). According to John Finnis, the "watershed" between the older tradition and the new had occurred by the time Suarez, whose major work was produced in the early seventeenth century, could write that "ius" meant "a kind of moral power which every man has, either over his own property or with respect to that which is due him" (quoted in Finnis 1980, pp. 206–207). And not long after, the influential work of Grotius had made the same claim: "ius" is "essentially something someone has, and above all (or at least paradigmatically) a power or liberty". In this way, the idea of a just relation or harmonious structure had been eclipsed as the primary meaning of "ius" since it was now "transformed by *relating it exclusively to the beneficiary* of the just relationship, above all to his doings and havings" (ibid., p. 207, original emphasis). This was a profound shift in meaning that would come to have long-lasting implications in the modern world.

And yet the full-scale predominance of rights was slow in coming. Under the influence of the Protestant Reformation, Haakonssen argues, there was still an "overwhelming emphasis on duty in modern natural law. Notions of virtue were to be interpreted in terms of duty; rights derived from duty; prima facie supererogatory acts were to be seen simply as special duties" (Haakonssen 1996, p. 26; I make no distinction in this book between the terms duty and obligation). Conceptually and doctrinally, obligations, and practices of obedience and supervision of belief, continued to dominate the core of everyday official and private engagements. Rights were acquiring a presence, especially the notion of natural rights, but the transformative and liberating impetus of the eighteenth-century rights revolutions were as yet unimagined.

In the following sections we will follow Haakonssen's insight by seeing how, despite the growth of rights discourse, obligations still continued to structure leading and influential legal and political theories. To do so we will consider accounts from three prominent British figures. These do not rank today in theoretical terms with Hobbes and Locke, but in their day two of them at least were far more powerful and influential than either of these. And the other is remembered best now for other reasons. They are, in turn, a king, a poet, and a judge.

With them we can identify three modes of obligation that are still with us. In the first, we see that government always claims *simultaneously* a right *and* an obligation to rule. In the hands of the king this plays out expressly through a series of double bonds that secure ties to God and, in terms of its explicit paternalism, asymmetric ties to subjects. In the second, we will see how obligations play a *constitutive* role in social relations generally, and – more particularly – how they may contribute to defining what it means to be an individual. And in the third we will address the importance of attending to the place of obligations within schemes of legal thinking and practice. Each of these three modes has, it will be argued in the next chapter, continuities even as the explicit rationalisations outlined here make way for other, new forms.

Divine rights and obligations

There is probably no more powerful exemplar of the doctrines of natural right being theorised in the seventeenth century than that of the divine right of kings which was being theorised *and* implemented. The leading proponent of the theory was, perhaps uncoincidentally, a king: James VI of Scotland (and from 1603 James I of England), "one of the most influential British political writers of the early modern period" (Somerville 1994, p. xv). His exposition of the doctrine of the divine right of kings formed part of a wider body of writings and political speeches which included *The Trew Law of Free Monarchies* (1598) and the internationally best-selling *Basilicon Doron* (the "Royal Gift", written in the same year though not published until 1603). Relying on Old Testament sources James argued that "Kings are not only God's lieutenants upon earth, and sit upon God's throne, but even by God himself they are called Gods"; "Kings are justly called Gods ...

they make and unmake their subjects: they have power of raising, and casting down: of life, and of death" (James 1994, p. 181). Because their power descended directly to them from God, they were accountable to God only; there was no earthly power to whom they were accountable. Despite its grounding in Scripture, as a political doctrine this was inevitably controversial. It challenged, for example, the analysis of James's brilliant teacher George Buchanan – whose writings, themselves controversial, were widely influential throughout Europe – who had argued in favour of a form of social contract according to which a monarch's power was constrained by the consent of the people who could, under certain circumstances, legitimately depose a tyrannical monarch (MacCormick 1982a). This was a controversy over the nature of power and its constraint that was far from academic: it would lead to civil wars and the deaths of tens of thousands of people including Charles I, James's son, who lost his head at the hands of the parliamentary authorities. It would endure throughout the century, and find resolution only with the Glorious Revolution with which John Locke's work is forever associated.

King James strenuously repudiated the view of kingship whereby a king could be held to account by his subjects, including those who held legislative or judicial office. But he did not reject the notion that he was constrained, indeed obligated as a king, in his reasoning and actions. What is significant for present purposes is how persistent and dominant the language of obligation was in James's schema. The *Trew Law*, for example, was sub-titled "the reciprocal and mutual duty betwixt a free king and his natural subjects" and in it he argued that

> [b]y the Law of Nature the King becomes a natural Father to all his lieges at his Coronation: and as the Father of his fatherly duty is bound to care for the nourishing, education, and virtuous government of his children; even so is the king bound to care for all his subjects.
>
> (James 1994, p. 65)

Thus natural duty founded his responsibilities, and the greater the power, the greater the responsibility to care for his subjects: the "higher that his seat is above [his subjects] the greater is his obligation to his maker" (James 1994, p. 83).

Basilicon Doron was originally intended as guidance to his son Henry, after whose early death his brother, the future Charles I, would become its recipient. In the first two (of three) parts, James's advice first addressed duties to God, and then the duties of kingship. He identified two double obligations that were central to these. The first of these double obligations was to God: "[F]irst for that he made you a man; and next for that he had made you a little GOD to sit on his throne, and rule over other men" (James 1994, p. 12). These are constitutive obligations: obligations that are part of what it means to have a particular status or role, in this case a king. In fulfilling the first of these James emphasised the biblical commands and prohibitions to be obeyed, which required dedicated obedience through prayer and action. The second is curious in that the king's right to rule over his subjects is derived from an obligation to God to so rule. In other words, James had both a right and an obligation to rule, and the former was derived from the latter. He again explained the position of the king as analogous to the way in which parents may be described (as they often still are) as having both a right *and* an obligation to care for their children. In this familial scenario, again drawing on Scriptural authority, ties of obligation went two ways. As Sir Edward Coke (to whom we will return shortly) put it, "Ligeance is the mutual bond and obligation between the King and his subjects ... as the subject oweth to the King his true and faithful ligeance and obedience, so the Sovereign is to govern and protect his Subjects" (*Calvin's Case*, 1608). Kings were "bound to rule" and protect their subjects, and subjects were bound to obey their king. It is this double relationship that explains the "mutual duty" between the two. Its "natural", unchanging, and indeed unchangeable aspect is promoted by the image of the protective father and dutiful child, a relationship which no human legislator could either create or destroy. As such, "natural ligeance or obedience of the subject to the Sovereign cannot be altered ... [it] is not due by the law or constitution of man" (*Calvin's Case*).

The second part of *Basilicon Doron* addresses the monarch's "duty in his office". This is a theme returned to in a speech to the English Parliament in 1610. James was no doubt trying to reassure his relatively new English subjects (particularly those with something, like wealth, to lose) that even although he was "accountable to none" on earth – for it was he who ultimately "speaks the law" – they should not be overly apprehensive. Reassurance is offered in the second of the "double obligations" which takes the form of "binding himself by a double oath to the observation of the fundamental laws of his kingdom". This double oath involves, first, "tacitly, as being a king, and so bound to protect as well the people, as the laws of his kingdom"; and, second, "expressly, by his oath at his coronation" (James 1994, p. 183). On the one hand, then, the "little god" is not bound to his people because *they* have bound him, but because the obligation to protect them comes, as we saw a moment ago, implicitly with the nature of the relationship and its specific roles. Any contrary view that might imply some kind of contractual arrangement which, if fundamentally breached by the king, could lead to his subjects having legitimate remedies against him was anathema. This was the kind of argument Buchanan had made 30 years earlier and John Locke would make again in the 1680s, according to which, in extreme circumstances of abuse of power "the people have a right to act as supreme" (Locke 1988, p. 428). This James of course rejected; it would be the equivalent of saying children had a right to rebel against their parents and this flatly contradicted the biblical commandment to "Honour thy father and thy mother". On the other hand, with kingship came the obligation to protect the laws and constitution of the land, its "fundamental laws". The king was therefore "bound to rule" through law and this was his way of making sure that the people were protected and all his obligations to them met consistently. As he said, "[A] king degenerates into a tyrant as soon as he leaves off to rule according to his laws" (James 1994, p. 183). Of course, they are *his* laws and there is no doubt, says James, that should any dispute arise as to their meaning or application where the power of decision lies: "[I]t is seditious in subjects to dispute what a king may do at the height of his power ... I will not be content that my power be disputed on" (ibid., p. 184).

It is well known that the great common law judge Sir Edward Coke took issue with at least one part of this view. He had argued, in the king's presence, that whilst it was true that the king had great learning, "his Majesty was not learned in the Lawes of his Realm of England" and that cases which arose under these were "not to be decided by naturall reason [which the king had], but by the artificiall reason and judgment of Law" (*Prohibitions del Roy*, 1607). Coke, the great propagandist of the common law, reported thus how he stood up to the king's power and in passing gave later common lawyers a memorable phrase in justifying their professional autonomy. What he did *not* report about the incident, however, was recorded via an eyewitness's account: after Coke had spoken, "his Majesty fell into that high indignation the like was never known in him, looking and speaking fiercely with bended fist, offering to strike him". Coke then "fell flat on all fours; humbly beseeching his Majesty to take compassion on him and to pardon him if he thought zeal had gone beyond his duty and allegiance" (quoted in Usher 1903, p. 670). It turned out that even the Chief Justice knew his place in the hierarchy of obligations.

We see clearly in these exchanges how the language of obligation is absolutely central to the meaning and exercise of constitutional power. Even at the high point of "divine right", the self-understanding of the monarch's authority took shape within a schema of obligations. There is no doubt in the king's mind, however, that in the hierarchy of obligations his subjects were lower down and just had to obey. But a good king, like a good father, would not act in any way to harm his children. The obligations were strict, and all the more so since it was God to whom they were ultimately owed. The language of binding was articulated vividly in the corporeal imagery of Coke himself, which captured the natural and constitutive force of obligation:

> Ligeance is a true and faithful obedience of the subject due to his Sovereign. As the ligatures or strings do knit together the joints of all the parts of the body, so doth ligeance joyn together the Sovereign and all his Subjects.
>
> (*Calvin's Case*)

What we note also in this is the implicit tracing of obligation's Latin roots through a continuous series of words and ideas, with the "*lig*" that signifies the tying common to obligation, ligeance, ligament (and, also, we should add, religion) that mesh together and culminate in the constitution of the body politic.

Considered in this light it is not quite true to say, as Michel Foucault did, that the history of "[r]ight in the West is the king's right" (Foucault 1984, p. 209). This description is at most only half correct. For the king's right was also the king's obligation, indeed, a series of obligations, and it would not have had the same ideological power or political effectiveness without these. That the king had the right to rule over his subjects was understandable only because it was at one and the same time his obligation to God to do so. And more to the point, the king's right only made sense as the history of *everyone else*'s obligations. These were layered, plural, and, certainly with respect to the religious cosmology within which they sat, necessary, comprehensive, and unyielding. The "king's right" would have been unrecognisable without them.

Donne on debt

To develop that last point let us turn now to a second aspect of early modern obligation: its effect on the constitution of the person. We will draw on a sermon by John Donne – the famous poet, lawyer, and clergyman – delivered when he was Dean of St Paul's Cathedral in London in the 1620s. It introduces a key concept in the realm of obligations and one to which we will return in a later chapter: debt. The text is Romans xiii.7: "Render therefore to all men their dues". In an opening line of possibly unsurpassed brilliance, Donne declaimed: "The largeness of this short text consists in that word, *therefore*". It continues: "[T]herefore because you have been so particularly taught your particular duties, therefore perform them, therefore practise them" (Donne 1623; quotes from Donne are from this text; no pagination is available). From this we can see there is both a logical ("therefore") and an experiential dimension (of learning, performance, and practice) to grasping the nature and power of obligations. It would be too simplistic to say that fulfilling obligations is an either/or matter. More is demanded of the dutiful, virtuous person than that would suggest. It is rather a *process*, of performance and practice, one that takes time and care and in and through which – crucially – the person is continuously being formed. And it is here that the language of debt becomes key.

Donne was a proponent of what is known as the "primordial-debt theory" (Graeber 2012, pp. 56ff.). This is the idea that human existence takes the form of a debt to God the creator (or, in different traditions, to the gods or ancestors or the spirits of the land, and so on). It is primordial in the sense that it is constitutive and inescapable: we are, just by being born, indebted to God for our very being. In Donne's terms, "[W]e are debtors of all that we have, and all that we are, to God; our well being, our very being is from Him". If this were not the case, Donne asks – the rhetoric appealing to a wide range of members of the congregation –

> from whom or from what, hath she stolen that face that is fair; or he that estate, that is rich; or that office, that commands others; or that learning, and those orders and commission, that preaches to others … If you owe nothing, from whom had you all these, all this?

The coming into existence of a person and everything they may have in this life – beauty, wealth, power, and so on – are all markers of this primordial debt; at this constitutive or ontological level there is no being without it being obliged. So whilst we have two other kinds of debt – those we have to our neighbours and those we have to ourselves – it is this debt to God that has the most distinctive and profound characteristics and consequences.

There can be little doubt that the language and significance of debt are especially potent articulations of obligations and that these would have resonated among the congregation of St Paul's. This was, no doubt, the point. And what everyone listening would also know is that debts required repayment. If debt is a burden on the debtor it is one that the creditor may call in at some point. Indeed, paying back the debt is precisely the way to release the debtor and have the burden lifted. But the debt to God differs in at least two respects. One is that the debt must somehow be honoured in a manner commensurate with its nature, which in this instance cannot of course be monetary. The other is that the nature of the debt is specified by the creditor, in this case God. What does this mean for the idea of repaying the debt?

In this context, the first part of the "payment" that is due, says Donne, is glory and praise. While these are indeed not monetisable, it does not mean the language of currency cannot be invoked to good effect. Quite the opposite. For glory and praise should be seen, says Donne, as "that money, which his own spirit mints, and coins in thee, and of his own bullion too ... Not to pay him, when he himself gives thee the money that must pay him" would be wrong. The second part of the "payment" that is due is prayer. And with this we come now to see a strange feature, the "essential difference peculiar to our debts to God". That is, "that we do not pay them, except we contract more; we grow best out of debt, by growing further in debt". What appears as paradoxical here is that the force of obligation and the obedience it calls for *demands more as more is paid*. Successful payment – praise, glory, and prayer – does not lift the burden of debt but succeeds only by failing.

There is again a double bond here, a double tie. That we owe all that we have to God puts us in his debt. But this, we now see, signifies something else: that we are obliged constantly, repeatedly, to pay for all this. We are not just indebted and able to sit still. We must act in response to this condition. We have obligations that can only be fulfilled by always living an obediential life, by constantly being obedient. The true force of this double bond derives from the fact that debts to God can never be settled. They are unpayable. *This* is what people must learn and act on: "*[T]herefore* because you have been so particularly taught your particular duties, therefore perform them, therefore practise them". It is not enough to acknowledge that the law God has "written on man's heart" is indelible and ever-present. For though this may be true, its legibility is at issue. As Stair vividly expressed it, "[T]hrough sin and evil custom the natural law on men's hearts was much defaced, disordered and erroneously deduced" (Stair, I.1.vii). Only by constantly living in obedience can this condition be addressed, and the effort be made at "un-defacing" and "re-ordering". It is for this reason that the practice and performance of obedience are necessary in grasping and living up to these obligations. Like repeatedly having to clean new graffiti off a "defaced" surface, obligatory performance is not carried out in a once and for all way – it is constant, for such is the consequence of man's sinful condition.

This explains the necessary, not the merely contingent, obligation of obedience which one cannot fulfil except by *being* obedient. The debt of existence cannot be paid off, at least in this life. If it could, here and now, if the debt could be settled once and for all, then the tie with God would be broken. For in a regular relationship between creditor and debtor, "[s]quaring accounts means that the two parties have the ability to walk away from each other" (Graeber 2012, p. 92). Yet why, it might be asked, if debts to God are by definition unpayable, do people bother at all? Why not accept God's gift of life and just get on with enjoying it? Why put in all the hard work of paying constant attention to fulfilling these obligations when they just reappear, like Sisyphus with his rock, over and over again? Or why not just be done with it and declare bankruptcy?

It is here that the mixture of obligation's religious, economic, and legal registers achieve their moment of fusion and power in Donne's sermon:

> [I]t is *turpe*, an infamous and ignominious thing not to pay debt; and, infamous and ignominious are heavy and reproachful words in the law; and the Gospel would add to that *turpe*, *impium*: it is not only an infamous, but an impious, an irreligious thing, not to pay debts.

The language of debt, common to law, religion, and economy combine here to secure the binding force of obligations operating on the minds, bodies, and, lest we forget, the souls of the people. And it is the last of these that contains the final and overwhelming impetus for unending obedience. A pious, virtuous Christian is promised one more thing, something extraordinary, albeit something that can only be received once they die: the promise of redemption. But Christ the "redeemer", as both Nietzsche and Graeber point out, also symbolises a reference back to economic and legal obligation. Because typically "redemption" refers to a debt or loan situation. And so Graeber concludes: "It is rather striking to think that the very core of the Christian message, salvation itself, the sacrifice of God's own son to rescue humanity from eternal damnation, should be framed in the language of a financial transaction" (Graeber 2012, p. 80). But this is exactly the source of the power of Donne's rhetoric, rare for its brilliance of expression but not for its conceptual ordering nor for its sentiment. The constitutive effects of debt and indebtedness are something to which we will return. For if many people today do not believe in religious salvation or "primordial debt" (in whatever form it takes), their non-belief will not save them from the manifest forms in which financial indebtedness – mortgage debts, credit card debts, student debts, and so on – continues to play a key role in the structuring of personal life and its opportunities or their lack. Even in our age of rights, economic forms and the financial institutions that sell and police debt combine with legal categories and enforcement mechanisms in the most profound and detailed ways to ensure, in Donne's words, that you are "taught your particular duties", and that you must continue to learn the same lesson over and over, albeit in a new key: "[T]herefore perform them, therefore practise them".

Obedience, freedom, engagement

Our third account of the priority of obligations comes from a judge, the founding figure of Scots Law, James Dalrymple, Viscount Stair (1619–1695). His major work, published in 1681 (Stair 1981), was a monumental intellectual achievement, synthesising natural law and protestant theology with Roman, canon, feudal, and local laws into a systematic and rational structure. As a foundational text in Scots Law, it holds a position similar to Blackstone's *Commentaries* in England and is still occasionally referred to by the courts. Stair became Lord President of the Court of Session, Scotland's top judge, but even holding such a powerful position did not make him immune from the insistent demands of loyalty oaths so prevalent in seventeenth-century political life. Refusing to swear an oath to the supremacy of the monarchy over the church he was forced to resign, went into exile, and was charged with treason. Only after his return from Holland with William of Orange during the Glorious Revolution was he able to resume his position as the head of the judiciary.

Our interest in Stair concerns the *place* of obligations within the overall structuring of his legal thought and practical doctrine. As we will see, rights were central to his account of positive law and legal practice, and by the end of the 1680s the English Bill of Rights and the Scottish Claim of Right (amongst other documents) showed clearly how much headway rights had made in political discourse. But Stair can be considered as something of a transitional figure in our account since the undoubted importance of legal rights only made sense for him within a structure of obligations.

While the French in 1789 came up with the winning slogan of "Liberté, Egalité, Fraternité", the Scots had a century earlier, in Stair's terms, established a more cautious Calvinist trio: "Obedience, Freedom and Engagement". In this schema primacy was given to those laws "written by the finger of God on men's hearts" which Stair called laws of equity or natural laws. There were three: the first was obedience, and its primary precept was that God is to be obeyed. It referred to

> that submission and sequacity of mind and will of man to the authority and will of his Maker, immediately obliging without any tie upon him by himself, intimate to him by the law of nature, light of reason and the conscience.
>
> (Stair 1981, I.1.xix (the references in this form in the following paragraphs are to Stair 1981))

Such obligations Stair termed "obediential" since they are "not by his own consent or engagement, nor by the will of man, but by the will of God". Of this kind Stair includes the "obligations betwixt husband and wife, parents and children, and the obligations of restitution, reparation and remuneration" as well as obligations "quasi ex-contractu" (ibid.). (With this last category, we might think that that finger of God had been well used to turning over the pages of Roman law textbooks!) "Obediential obligations" thus had an inescapable priority and could be differentiated from "conventional" obligations, that is, those created through human convention.

The second principle of equity is freedom. This holds "that man is a free creature, having power to dispose of himself and all things, in so far as by his obedience to God he is not restrained" (I.1.xviii). Man, for Stair, "is by nature free in all things, where this obedience [to God] has not tied him, until he oblige himself" and hence "where obedience ends, there freedom begins" (I.1.xx). The third principle of equity is thus "engagement". Engagement "begins where freedom ends; it being our voluntary obliging of ourselves where by nature we are free" (I.1.xxi). Such freedom as we have can be used therefore to bind us in turn, but now according to our own choices, such as when we decide to enter into contracts to bind our actions to some future performance. In Stair's schema then freedom is located *between* two sets of obligation – "obediential" and those created by human engagement.

As reasoned deductions or *determinationes* from general principles of natural laws human laws were added according to the three principles of positive law: society, property, and commerce. In the Christian framework, since man is a fallen being and liable to corrupt and sinful practices, he needs actively to secure peaceful social relations to avoid the possibility of constant conflict and injury. Hence he must direct himself "to make up societies of men that they may mutually defend one another, and to procure to one another their rights" (I.1.xviii). The first principle of positive law is therefore "society", the need, as in social contract theory, to create and sustain peaceful society. Positive law must work therefore to deliver a tolerable sociability, to guarantee stability and peace in order that society can flourish. The second principle – property – is required to "set clear limits to every man's property" and the third, commerce, "to maintain traffic and commerce among themselves and with others". Hence the aim of the three principles is, according to Stair, "the maintenance, flourishing, and peace of society, the security of property and the freedom of commerce" (ibid.). Now we reach the conclusion of Stair's structural edifice. For the principles of equity are "the efficient cause of rights and laws", and the principles of positive law are the "ends for which laws are made, and rights constitute and ordered" (I.1.xviii). For Stair then, the "formal and proper object of [positive] law are the rights of men" (I.1.xxii). And since it is "the prime interest of men ... to enjoy their rights" (I.1.xv) positive law secures these in an orderly way in a world where men have been corrupted by sin.

The position of rights in Stair's overall framework was thus clearly circumscribed. Rights were indeed the "object of positive law" but they were not originary in the way that "obediential obligations" were. This was not merely a matter of conceptual organisation, but had real implications as Stair the lawyer was all too aware (Campbell 1954). Thus, for example, with reference to the law of property, obligations were, he said, "in nature and time for the most part anterior to, and inductive of, rights real of dominion and property" (III.1). Such prioritisation of obligation according to this schema thus had practical consequences: if "the treatment and the status of obligations [is] prior to the treatment and the status of property ... obligations are imposed upon and constrain the property owner" (MacIntyre 1988, p. 230).

Stair was working within a reasonably conventional Christian natural law framework, in which "law is the dictate of reason" (I.1.i), and hence his ideas owe a good deal to a tradition going back through Grotius earlier in the seventeenth century to the Reformation and beyond. While the priority of obligation was to be found in the structure of religious belief and doctrine, the role of these in the intellectual systematisation of a legal system and its detailed practical precepts was not a mere frontispiece offering embellishment. As Dot Reid puts it, "Stair was intent not only in creating a rational system of law, but one which was godly in character and would, in turn, yield godly Scottish citizens" (Reid 2008, p. 190). This intention should not be understated. Nor would its presence have been thought in any way odd in its day. Obediential obligations formed the grounding for conventional obligations, which together formed the weave of duties, loyalties, and in turn the freedoms and rights that social life demanded and offered. They made up the bonds of society, of sociality, whose obligations defined family, friendship, community, and the sense of conscientiousness, dedication, and virtue in practical and spiritual activities. Obediential obligations did not gain their force from positive laws, or from human agreements. Yet they were the mainspring of justice and equity. They were indeed what rights would memorably be declared to be in a different context 100 years later: they were inalienable.

Thus what grounded human relations and their political and legal institutions was not some idea of a "right to rights" as William Galbraith Miller (1903, pp. 132, 204), and later Hannah Arendt more famously, described it. Instead, it is the priority of obligations that provides for the *possibility* of rights. Two implications of this can be drawn out. First, that there was no sense of an individual or of an individual's freedom that would have made sense separately from or prior to such ties. The idea that "man was born free" was a notion still awaiting expression. Even Stair's contemporary Thomas Hobbes, the arch-individualist, knew that his idea of a state of nature in which individuals existed purely on their own, without social constraint in a war of all against all, was only a thought experiment required to ground his theory of the strong state; "there never was such a time", he admits (Hobbes 1996, p. 89). Second, basic individual passions and desires were still seen as in need of transformation; they were not yet the raw data which social institutions had to record and respond to. In other words, this kind of society was not yet "after virtue" (MacIntyre 1985). Learning and practising the virtues, and the constant fulfilment of obligations, were the assumptions within which people existed and their social and moral well-being developed. The ideas of individualism and preference satisfaction would have made no sense in this context.

Writers such as Stair were thus arguably at the end of something rather than the beginning. Commenting on certain similarities between

Stair and Locke, Neil MacCormick suggested that, among other things, the notion of a social contract was even by this time

> an archaic doctrine, which gains credibility from the traditional and feudal interpretations of social order, rather than looking forward to the emergent order of bourgeois or commercial society. Indeed, it is the high priests of commercial society, such as Hume, Bentham, and above all Adam Smith who pour most scorn on the theory.
>
> (MacCormick 1982a, p. 75)

The latter part of this observation is undoubtedly correct, even if, as we will see in a moment, there was still revolutionary potential left in the idea of the social contract. For the priority of obligations was increasingly to give way, at least in the dominant legal and political theory and practice, to the power and functioning of rights. This did indeed coincide with the new dictates of "commercial society", which would increasingly come to treat individualism and economic gain as the dominant values that provided the measure of social life. In this newly emergent form of social organisation the prominence and fluency of public discourses of obligation receded. But as we have seen, in the historical and comparative perspective outlined so far, this coming situation would be an exception. As Samuel Moyn recently put it, "Our age of rights, lacking a public language of duties, is a historical outlier" (Moyn 2017, p. 164). Yet in the next chapter we will see how, if that discourse did indeed begin to ebb, the presence and labour of obligations did not.

3 Shifting priorities
Into the modern

Revolutionary rights and subterranean continuities

One of the defining features of modernity is commonly taken to be the rise of the "individual" as a new social presence. Where previously people were people only through relationships or status, which always had primacy, being an "individual" who stood outside these was not a plausible or endurable condition in either theory or practice. Aristotle's insight had cast a long shadow: to exist outside society was to be either a beast or a god. In the older traditions, as Hannah Arendt memorably expressed it, "[t]he question is never whether an individual *is* good but whether his conduct is good for the world he lives in. In the center of interest is the world and not the self" (Arendt 2003, p. 151, emphasis in original). The idea therefore of the "individual" who pre-existed social order and who had individual entitlements in the form of rights would have been thought very strange.

And yet in modernity it was precisely this strange idea that began to gain prominence. By the eighteenth century an older tradition of natural law had given birth to the idea that individuals had natural and inalienable rights, and this idea had gained not only prominence but revolutionary momentum. Natural law, "'which had been for nearly two thousand years a harmless maxim, almost a commonplace of morality' was converted into 'a mass of dynamite which shattered an ancient monarchy and shook the European continent'" (D'Entreves 1951, p. 10, quoting James Bryce). Such was its success, however, that a central problem for legal and political theory became: how to socialise such an anti-social figure? This was in one sense a false problem: no-one (except beasts or gods) *really* existed separately from that web of expectations, obligations, and reciprocities that society and its many groupings consisted of. But that this figure was a fiction did not mean it did not have to be addressed; successful inventions of the human

Shifting priorities 37

mind, whether gods or corporations, usually require a great deal of work to integrate them into mental and social patterns in order to understand their potential and their implications.

There can be no doubt that a major part of this new thinking was a response to the dangers that *not* postulating individuals' rights involved. The king or the state or powerful social actors such as the Church could use their power, as we saw earlier, to define and control the lives of their subjects (and even lay claim to their afterlives) and could do so without any form of meaningful accountability *to* their subjects. Instead, such powers were hedged in with *unenforceable* commitments such as the paternalistic sentiments of kings or promises of salvation in the life hereafter. By contrast, establishing that individuals had rights, such as those to a private life, to property, to assembly, to free speech or freedom of conscience, and so on, meant the king and the state could no longer act with impunity. Instead of their obligations being a matter of *noblesse oblige*, rights could make them enforceable. King James's nightmare would have come true: the children could be justified in speaking back to their superiors, constraining them, and even, in the worst case, rebelling against them. This changed everything. Moreover, these rights – or at least those rights that meant most to those who had most to lose if they lost them; typically property rights and those who held lots of property – were protections whose enforceability, ironically dependent on the state apparatus that might also endanger them, had transformative potential by providing new kinds of restraint.

In this sense, the rise of the discourse and practice of rights was equally about the generation and re-allocation of obligations. If the sovereign's arbitrary power was to be curtailed this would only happen if rights were recognised and obligations effectively distributed and administered. The development of rights is at one and the same time therefore a development of constraints through obligation and practices of obedience. Without the power of these constraints, operationalised through a far greater number and range of enforceable legal obligations, and without the constitution of subjects and officials as law-bound actors in legally defined roles, rituals, procedures, and offices, claims to enforceable rights would barely have been meaningful at all.

So if individuals had rights which belonged to them as individuals, and each individual had these equally (at least in theory) the problem became two-fold: how to integrate these individuals (and their rights) and how to establish an authority that could affirm, protect, and legitimately enforce individuals' rights claims, and adjudicate on disputes that arose from their breach or from clashes among them. Or, to put it slightly differently: how could coercive authority *over* individuals be reconciled with the rights and entitlements *of* these individuals? Some answers to this question still invoked older "natural law" traditions, going back to the writings of St Thomas Aquinas, about the state being the ultimate expression and facilitator of the common good. Others, like David Hume, gave a more sceptical, atheist, but ultimately pragmatic account of how utility solved the problem: government over individuals was legitimate because it was useful in protecting justice and people's rights and interests (particularly those to property), adding importantly – and carefully, for he was no political radical – that the artificial (as opposed to natural) virtue of justice required that a new "factitious" obligation had to be formulated: "Obedience is a new duty which must be invented to support that of Justice; and the ties of equity must be corroborated by those of allegiance" (Hume 1987, p. 38).

But the most influential of all the answers given to this problem were those that inherited and updated an alternative model rooted in the consent of the governed. Although there were important variations, the narrative essentially involved this: we should imagine individuals without government, in a state of nature, coming together to agree to the political and legal conditions within which they were to live. This agreement, or social contract, would provide a legitimacy that solved the problem of individualism, rights, and coercive authority. Having achieved prominence in the work of Hobbes and Locke in the seventeenth century (and *pace* MacCormick) this model took on a renewed and revolutionary impetus in the eighteenth century. The works of Rousseau and Kant in particular deepened the sophistication of the model, and these have had an enduring resonance in political and legal thought and practice.

If there were variations in these writings, and there were many, what they all had in common was this: that rights required restraints. In other words, by voluntarily submitting to a common authority freedom entailed obligation. Hobbes's version was typically precise: "In the act of submission, consisteth both our obligation, and our liberty" (Hobbes 1996, p. 150). Unfettered freedom was no freedom at all. That was why the state of nature was problematic and had to be left. Thereafter rights could protect freedom, but freedom required the unfreedom of obligation too: it required law to restrict and restrain, to impose obligations that could be enforced. These included obligations not only of citizens to each other and all of them to the state, but of the state to citizens. If individuals had rights and these individuals and their rights were to be protected from arbitrary interference by others (and because of their power, the king or the state in particular), then that protection must be grounded in the reciprocally enforceable guarantees of a plethora of obligations owed towards these individuals based on the rights they had. Only with the regular observance of such obligations by citizens and the state could individual freedom be meaningful.

Two key observations can be made about this model, one concerning the nature of sovereignty and the other with respect to remedies. The first is that (at least on some accounts of social contract) sovereign coercive power could be promoted as legitimate because, in theory, it was the people that ruled themselves. "Autonomy" means literally "self-rule" and so *collective* autonomy meant that all the people ruled themselves all together. In this way it was legitimate for people to be bound by the law if they were the people who made the law. This solved the problem of how rights and coercive authority were compatible since obligations would not diminish freedom but deliver it, and we will return to this shortly. It followed from this (again, at least on some accounts) that when some person or group of people usurped that commonality and equivalence, legitimate remedial action could be taken against them justified by the claim of popular sovereignty and the expectations people legitimately had in the protection of their rights. In circumstances where a sovereign power seriously and serially abused this idea then, as Jefferson put it in declaring colonial secession from the British state, "it is the right of the people to alter or abolish it and to institute new government". Indeed, such was the power of the idea of the coincidence of authorship of, and obligation to, the law that it was not merely *a right* to rebellion that was claimed; where a people were being severely maltreated like this, continued Jefferson, "it is their right, *it is their duty* to throw off such government" (Jefferson 1776, emphasis added). Right does not correlate to *another's* duty here; they exist in the same agent, the people, who are duty-bound to make good their right.

The most theoretically sophisticated accounts of social contract were those offered by Rousseau and Kant. For both, the role of the sovereign state was not just a matter of interest and utility, as Hume had argued, but a matter of the very constitution of the *idea* of rights. "It is not some fact", Kant argued, "that makes coercion through public law necessary" (Kant 1996, p. 123). Rather, there was a transcendental dimension to their formulations, captured in Rousseau's observation that "[t]he strongest is never strong enough always to be the master unless he transforms strength into right and obedience into duty" (Rousseau 1973, p. 184). It was precisely in such metamorphoses that conceptual legitimacy transcended the realm of facts. Kant drew in part on Rousseau's work, and we will turn briefly to his account here.

Although Kant would vigorously denounce the idea of a right to rebel against an existing government as theoretically incoherent (no matter how despotic that government was), his influence on thinking about autonomy, equality, and rights is difficult to overstate. Kant was concerned with ascertaining the *conditions* according to which everyone's freedom and autonomy could be respected equally. If violence and powerful interests were not to be decisive – if might was not to make right, in other words – a theory of legitimate authority was needed to explain and guarantee by coercion everyone's freedom equally. Using social contract thinking as well as Rousseau's notion of the general will, Kant's analysis proposed a solution grounded in the reciprocal granting of rights and duties under a universal law. As explained by Korsgaard, Kant's overarching question is: "[H]ow is coercive political authority possible? His answer is that ... The state must embody the general will of the people to the reciprocal enforcement of those rights which constitute the freedom of everyone" (Korsgaard 2008, pp. 240–241). This was, as Korsgaard notes, a "transcendental" argument about the conditions of *possibility* of such authority. It was only in these a priori terms that the condition of autonomy could be elucidated and "the freedom of the agent could coexist with the freedom of every other in accordance with a universal law" (Kant 1996, p. 188). It followed from this that since it was *only* in such a "juridical condition" that people's freedom and rights could be equally and reciprocally guaranteed, that people had a duty to enter into this condition and could indeed be forced into doing so; in Rousseau's terms, they could be "forced to be free". But because this achieved the "united will of the people", it "*cannot* do anyone wrong by its law" (Kant 1996, p. 125). The coincidence of freedom and obligation was therefore legitimate since "*lawful* freedom [is] the attribute of obeying no other law than that to which he has given his consent" (ibid., emphasis in original).

But, as Kant noted, and as historical experience bore out only too vividly, this relationship – in which freedom meant obeying only laws to which one has consented – was *in practice* highly asymmetrical. The reality was that only a few had rights to create the law, while *everyone* had the obligation to obey it. And this signalled – and for our purposes, still signals – something of profound significance: obligations were doing far more work than rights in the political and legal organisation of society. In Kant's *Metaphysics of Morals*, we encounter at this point a pause in the theoretical analysis, a moment where an intrusion of realism needed to be addressed and Kant, rigorous if nothing else, had to square up to it. He noted that while the equal freedom of all citizens – as collective self-determination – was the ideal, in reality this was not the case. This could be explained, however, by differentiating between active and passive citizenship. This distinction was crucial not just in explanatory terms, but because it also structured and *legitimated* a reality whose discriminations were capable of being acted upon as justified, with severe consequences for many.

The distinction between active and passive citizenship came down to the difference between those who wrote the laws and had to obey them and those who did not write the laws and yet must still obey. Those in the position of equivalence – active citizens who had a reciprocity of rights and obligations – were contrasted to those who did not benefit from such equivalence; those – many more in fact – *passive* citizens who had the full set of obligations, but not those of rights. Kant acknowledged a certain hypocrisy in this position since "the concept of a passive citizen *seems* to contradict the concept of a citizen as such" (Kant 1996, p. 126, emphasis added). But it was explainable, he argued, by the qualification that stated that people were only "fit to vote" if they were not dependent on the will of others. Children, for example, said Kant, are to be understood as dependents in this way and so are not the equals of adults when it came to fitness to vote. They were in this sense passive citizens: they ought to *obey* rather than join in writing the rules for everyone's behaviour. Once they reached the age of adulthood, that aspect of passivity would no longer apply.

But seldom can the claim that something merely "seems" contradictory have been so deftly, then brutally, deployed. It may be that with respect to children, particularly young children, that such a condition is appropriate to designating them unfit to vote and thus liable to obey but not write the laws. But this criterion does not only apply to them. So who else is excluded from active citizenship? Kant gives a list:

> [A]n apprentice ... a domestic servant (as distinguished from a civil servant) ... all women ... the woodcutter I hire in my yard; the blacksmith in India ... as compared with the European carpenter or blacksmith ... the tenant farmer ...

People in these categories were all unfit to vote. They were "mere underlings of the commonwealth because they have to be under the direction or protection of other individuals, and so do not possess civil independence" (Kant 1996, p. 126).

Not just children then; but certain classes of workers, foreign races, *all* women. Underneath the transcendental categories, underneath the veneer of philosophical justifications of freedom and equality, there is the reality of unfreedom and inequality that Kant (in one sense to his credit) does not disavow. But he is not yet finished with this thought. For he adds of this inequality that "this dependence ... is in no way opposed to their freedom and equality *as men*, who together make up a people" (ibid., emphasis in original). In other words, their natural or human equality – the fact that they are *human beings* – means they are still equally subject to the force of the law: they still have obligations to obey the law. And it is precisely their natural "freedom" as humans which makes them, unlike animals who have no such similar capacities, capable of being held liable for breaching them. This confirms the sociologist Georg Simmel's insight into the "peculiar structure of authority"; that it

> presupposes, in a much higher degree than is usually recognised, a freedom on the part of the person subjected to authority. Even where authority seems to "crush" him, it is based not *only* on coercion or compulsion to yield to it.
> (Simmel 1964, p. 183, emphasis in original)

Hence it is *freedom as liability to obligations* that is doing the real work here. Perhaps only beasts or gods could legitimately escape this; all the passive citizens could not.

Here was the reality of eighteenth-century revolutionary social contract and its theories of legitimacy and equality: all are equal in liability to obligations, but not all are equal in rights. Obligations fall hardest on those – *servants, Indian races ... all women* – who are told they are not active citizens; who are, by contrast only passive – *except* in obligations where they are more active than anyone. This was the "universalist" modus operandi of the European Enlightenment. In contrast to the theologically framed rights of the seventeenth century, which in the main had treated obligation in the public domain as prior, its self-image would see it as inaugurating a great new age of rights where freedom, not obligation, would achieve priority. In reality, obligations had just gone underground, there to do as much work as ever but largely now hidden from the light of reasoned discourse. There was one hope though, one spark of light in Kant's account: "natural freedom" also contained the possibility that a citizen could "work his way up from this passive condition to an active one" (Kant 1996, p. 126). That might apply to a rich white male child when he grew into a rich white male adult. But most people would not grow up to be this, for obvious reasons. For them, passive citizenship was their lot, and the removal of this status lay a long way in the future.

New priorities

The splitting off of autonomy for some – the self-rule where rights and obligation coincide as freedom – and its denial for the rest, who are ruled but have no participation in "self"-rule, legitimates the persistence of inequality despite the promise of equality. Wherever that asymmetry continues today, this remains the case. To believe otherwise, to believe there is an equality of equivalence of rights and obligation when the condition of autonomy is not met would require believing something absurd, a kind of Stockholm syndrome for political theory: "To impose obligations to sustain discriminatory practices upon members of a subordinated or dominated group, we would have to believe that it is both rational and necessary for the oppressed to support their own repression" (Kerruish and Hunt 1992, p. 237). And yet this was the reality of the Enlightenment project in its post-revolutionary practice, where the many were still dominated by the few and the promise of equality was proffered but not met. Rights were limited in their distribution but obligations fell equally or even more intensely on those who had little or (more usually) no say in their formulation. In this section we will consider two developments here with respect to the role of obligations. The first addresses the ways in which the shift to rights was played out in reality. The second shows that despite, in one sense, as we have just noted, obligations having gone subterranean, in another sense a new source of obligation had emerged as prior. There had been, in other words, a structural substitution of religion as the enframing level in the hierarchy of obligation and its replacement by another – and still dominant – obligatory form.

Kant's recognition of the passivity designated to most races, to women, and to many workers was borne out forcefully by nineteenth-century practices. For this was also the age of empire par excellence. By the end of the civil war in the United States, the violent removal of over 12 million men, women, and children from Africa to forced labour camps in the Americas had been going on for hundreds of years and enabled vast fortunes to be made by those who benefitted from exploiting human labour to such an unprecedented degree. (The British government in 1833 borrowed such a vast sum of money to end slaveholding in the Empire that the debt was not paid off until 2015. In a contemporary manifestation of the asymmetries we are tracing here, the debt obligations of the British government were owed to the slave *owners* – not one penny of this sum was deemed owed to freed slaves or their kin in compensation for their brutal treatment; rather, it compensated slave owners for *their* losses (Manjapra 2018.) Throughout the century, extensive colonial land thefts and consolidations by Western powers were accompanied by genocidal acts, all of which had been designated lawful by the colonisers. A judgement of the British Privy Council in a 1919 case captures some of the essence and spirit of the thinking behind this:

> Some tribes are so low on the scale of social organization that their usages and conceptions of rights and duties are not to be reconciled with the institutions or the legal ideas of civilized society. Such a gulf cannot be bridged.
>
> (*In re Southern Rhodesia*, quoted in *Mabo v State of Queensland*
> (1992) para 38)

If such bridging was not possible, then what linked the colonisers themselves throughout the Empire was not simply force and violence but something, as we noted Kant had said, transcendental: law. As Lord Shaw put it in a speech to lawyers in Canada in 1922, the law was

> an elevating, harmonising and binding force ... It is in this way that law, as a Link of Empire comes to be a very sacred thing. By force of reason and principle, law is lifted to the level of true majesty as the friend of progress. It gives liberty and individualism among the nations their chance, and receives back from them an enlightened gratitude or co-operation.
>
> (Shaw 1923, p. 118)

It might be difficult to surpass this as a summation of the "modern, enlightened" colonial attitude. The problem was not that this was all, and only, in Lord Shaw's and his fellows' minds, divorced from the realities of dispossession and degradation. It was rather that this overarching sensibility formed a principle of rule that could do no wrong. As Karuna Mantena puts it, "That empire could be simultaneously cause and cure for the crisis of native society became an alibi for permanent imperial rule" (Mantena 2010, p. 177).

The experience of indigenous peoples throughout the empire was the consequence in material terms of this principle. With respect to land and culture they suffered

> deprivation of the religious, cultural and economic sustenance which the land provides, vested the land exclusively in the control

of the Imperial authorities without any right to compensation and made the indigenous inhabitants intruders in their own homes and mendicants for a place to live.

(Brennan CJ, in *Mabo*, para 28)

In all this the asymmetry between rights and obligations we noted in Kant's work played, in various incarnations, a continuing role. But to grasp just how important the specific role of obligations was in this we may refer briefly to the work of HLA Hart who captured this point expertly, if perhaps unintentionally, in describing the conditions for the existence of a legal system in his influential book *The Concept of Law*.

For Hart a legal system exists where there is a union of primary and secondary rules. Primary rules are rules of obligation; secondary rules are about primary rules in that they confer powers to regulate the conditions according to which legal rules are recognised, changed, and adjudicated on. Rules impose obligations, says Hart, when the "general demand for conformity is insistent and the social pressure brought to bear upon those who deviate or threaten to deviate is great" (Hart 1961, p. 84). But not all societies have legal systems. According to Hart, "primitive societies", which are a "simple form of social life", "live by such primary rules alone". They are, he says, "pre-legal" (ibid., pp. 89, 91) and as such seem to offer less insight into the study of law than the rules of cricket, to use one of Hart's favourite examples. This account captures precisely, for it is entirely consistent with, the colonial mentality that *treats* "primitive societies" as without law, and hence liable *only* to obligations from the colonial power. As Brennan described the racist doctrine of terra nullius on which basis Australia was founded, "The indigenous people of a settled colony were thus *taken to be* without laws, without a sovereign and primitive in their social organisation" (*Mabo*, para 36, emphasis added). In historical terms, in other words, the "primitive" was the *construct* of the "civilized" legal system, and from the point of view of the colonisers that constructed reality meant that the obligations imposed and obedience demanded by the colonial power was all that colonised peoples *could* have. To that extent, it did in fact match indigenous peoples' experience: treated as passive citizens (or subjects), as human, if barely so, but enough to be held responsible for their behaviour – to be rounded up, removed from their lands, incarcerated, forced to work, and worse.

Hart's account of the existence of a legal system subscribes to the doctrine of legal positivism. This argues that the validity of "civilized" laws has no necessary connection to moral values. Where horrific acts thus occur in the name of such laws, there is no reason not to call this a legal system so long as the criteria of validity of the system are met. These were two-fold: first, it was necessary that the *officials* of the system treated the laws as valid under what Hart termed the system's rule of recognition. The attitudes of all the rest of the people who were subject to the law had no bearing on this aspect. In practice this meant that the "centrally organized power may well be used for the oppression of numbers with whose support it can dispense" (ibid., p. 198). The existence of law does not require their support for the law to be valid (which anyway would require the legal equivalent of the Stockholm syndrome where they are being oppressed). Instead, legal validity needs only one thing of all of them: their obedience. Hence the second condition for the existence of a legal system: that "those rules of behaviour which are valid according to the system's ultimate criteria of validity must be generally obeyed" (ibid., p. 113). Hart thus encapsulates remarkably accurately the asymmetry we have traced through Kant's account of the distinction between active and passive citizens, setting this out explicitly in terms of obligations and obedience, and unerringly describing the capability of the lawful oppression of populations that was built into the very "concept of law" and the definition of a valid legal system.

This was the reality of "Enlightenment" rights and "civilised" legal systems in the empire and domestically: officials defined the law and this sanctioned obligations of obedience on the general populace. But if equality of rights and obligations was a lie, it was one that few people could plausibly believe in given their experience. As we noted in the Introduction it was Hart who identified the "figure of a bond binding the person obligated" as haunting "much legal thought". One need not be a psychoanalyst to understand that this haunting, from the perspective just outlined, might be populated by the bodies and souls for whom lawful freedom – "that attribute of obeying no other law than that to which he has given his consent" – was neither attained nor attainable.

That this structure persisted even as more people were brought into the range of rights-holder position – which was usually the result of more or less peaceful struggle *against* such inclusion – showed the resilience of the institutional force of the legal system and the interests that dominated it. As was clear throughout the twentieth century in the cases of race and gender, from the point of view of those who gained most from the status quo, current conditions were usually argued to be non-negotiable. Still, the idea that "all men are created equal" and that the principle of good government should be based in the consent of the governed had gained something of a foothold.

Even when this principle achieved formal endorsement, however, as it did slowly, unevenly, and intermittently in the course of the modern era, a split between the contradictory realities of equal citizenship and widespread social and economic inequality continued. We will return to aspects of why and how this might be so in a later chapter. But for now, consider how Edwin Cameron, a leading judge in the South African Constitutional Court, recently articulated this split when he compared the current South African constitution to the system of legally authorised apartheid it superseded. "What is different is that we have a legitimate government, a legitimate legal system, and a legitimate constitution ... South Africa has the world's most enlightened constitution ... a functioning democracy, rooted in popular will, a credible judiciary" (Cameron 2016, pp. 359–360). In this sense, the promise of Kant's version of autonomy as self-rule had been instantiated, and all the hallmarks of the equality of rights and obligations constitutionally enshrined. And yet, Cameron continued: "Today, South Africa manifests rampant inequality, dispossession, injustice and exclusion" (359). The co-existence of these contradictory observations – an enlightened constitution and democratically legitimated government juxtaposed with extensive inequality and injustice – begs the question of why such inequality does not invalidate the legitimacy of the constitution? Does its being "rooted in" the will of all the people carry sufficient weight to make the dispossession and exclusion of many immune from registering constitutionally on the basis that "the united will of the people ... cannot do anyone wrong *by its law*" (as we noted earlier in Kant's account)? Are rights and obligations really evenly distributed even in a democracy?

Post-Enlightenment there was – and still is, as the case of South Africa clearly demonstrates – a great disconnect between lived experience and the notion of equal rights protected equally for all. For the vast majority of people, enlightened ideas of consensual rule and equality before the law were not "self-evident truths". Rather, what *was* self-evidently true was that most of them lived in varying degrees of enforced inequality and indignity. Kant's description of the categories of passive citizens continued to do its work of exclusion from rights and inclusion through intensely enforced practices of obligation and obedience: non-white races, workers, all women. In the United States, for example, slavery was replaced by an apartheid system that would continue formally until the 1960s and informally thereafter. More generally, where problems of poverty, exclusion, and discrimination were coming to be addressed, they were addressed patchily and again usually in face of opposition from conservative forces resisting change.

Hence, even as equality came to be recognised in the political realm, the central problem identified by Edwin Cameron's observations on contemporary South Africa was already clear. Surveying Britain in the mid-twentieth century Aneurin Bevan summed up the challenge many faced: "How [did] wealth persuade poverty to use its political freedom to keep wealth in power?" (Bevan 1952, p. 4). In all this the distorting image law gave of the economic realm played a key role. And a significant aspect of this was a transformation in the nature and place of obligations in the hierarchies of social thought and practice.

A structural substitution

The notion that individuals and individualism had appeared in a way distinctive to modernity contained some truth. But this too had to be tempered by reality. To some extent individuals – some more than (many) others – had been liberated from some of the strictures of the seventeenth century's age of obligation. But even this had happened in a very particular way, one that challenges the notion of the individual abstract rights holder becoming the new atomic element of society. For as well as the formal exclusions of the passive citizenry, the particular form liberation of the individual took was clear. Writing of eighteenth-century England, MacIntyre described this well: social relationships linked

> not individuals as such, but individuals identified in terms of the resources which they possess and upon which they can draw in contributing to the exchanges which constitute social life. So the individual as propertied, as property owner or as propertyless, is the unit of social life, and the rules governing the distribution and exchange of property are an integral part of the rules constituting the system of social exchanges. Status and power within the system depend on the ownership of property.
> (MacIntyre 1988, p. 216)

Two points are important to note about this. First, that even where some form of democratisation began to deliver on the promise of an equivalence of rights and obligations with respect to the legitimacy of state power and the limits placed on it through the constitution and laws of the state, the structuring of forms of association reliant on economic and private law forms (centrally property and contract) held out no such promise of equivalence. What existed instead was a continued asymmetry – rights for some and obligations for all – but in a mutated form. For the real working conditions of labourers, not only adult males, but of children and women, were those of *necessity*, not freedom; "For how many capitalist enterprises would remain", asks Lordon rhetorically, "if people were freed from necessity?" (Lordon 2014, p. 127). These conditions bound men, women, and children to work practices, departure from which would mean unemployment and starvation. All these aspects of "civil society" within which people lived their lives were thus constituted by a range of dependencies that were defined essentially not by rights but by obligations and practices of obedience. In so far as this reality did not form part of the dominant discourse about the increased importance of rights it is possible to talk about obligations going subterranean. But this alone would not tell the whole story. Because the second point to note is that under such circumstances a new form of obligation became prominent. It is to this claim that we now need to turn in more detail.

One way to understand what had occurred was to see that a structural substitution had taken place. We saw in Chapter 2 how in the seventeenth century writers had conceptualised the constitution of subjectivity in the language of pre-existing obligations: kingly power and subjects' loyalties as constituted by obligations to God; subjectivity as a matter of indebtedness (for Donne) and those precepts written on men's hearts which together signified (in Stair's terms) that in the hierarchy of obedience, freedom and engagement, freedom was best understood as existing between two sets of obligation. But as the religious superstructure gave way, at least in the sense that it was no longer the publicly dominant organising principle of political society and state regulation, it might be expected that freedom would emerge now at the top of the hierarchy. With the priority of religious obligations waning in terms of political legitimation, in other words, and religious belief retreating to the private realm of individual conscience and freedom of religion – protected from (and by) the state through individual rights – a genuine liberation would seem to have occurred.

But viewed from an alternative perspective, the priority of religious obligations was in reality replaced by a new form: the precepts of the market. Marx had captured this vividly when he described the colonial system as

> the "strange God" who perched himself side by side with the old divinities of Europe on the altar, and one fine day threw them all overboard with a shove and a kick. It proclaimed the making of profit as the ultimate and the sole purpose of mankind.
> (Marx 1976, p. 918)

As industrial capitalism became the dominant mode of economic production in the nineteenth century, and as it spread within individual countries and throughout the world under the flags and whips of the imperial powers, its force replaced and in fact replicated some key features of religious belief. Across the domains of knowledge, value, and the constitution of subjectivity this new "strange God" came to impose its obligations at all levels of social life.

The language of religion is not out of place here for a number of reasons. Like religion, capitalism offers to make sense of the world and humanity's place within it. It seeks to be comprehensive in its reach – albeit, like religion, from a particular perspective – in providing categories of understanding and action ranging from the designation of what is to be counted as valuable to the meaning and measurement of progress and even the definition of time and space. And it provides a language and mode of organisation that sets ground rules for success, overseen by visionaries and ministering officials that propel the spreading of the word. As the Harvard theologian Harvey Cox noted recently in his book *The Market as God*,

> Faith in the workings of markets actually takes the form of a functioning religion, complete with its own priests and rituals, its own doctrines and theologies, its own saints and prophets, and its own zeal to bring its gospel to the world and win converts everywhere.
> (Cox 2016, p. 6)

The reason why this is best understood as a "structural substitution" is that the precepts of the market economy provided the structuring principles *within* which freedom had now to be understood. Freedom had not, it turned out, been liberated. The obediential obligations Stair had written about as having priority ahead of freedom had merely been replaced by a new set of "obediential obligations"; those, so to speak, "written on men's hearts" by the new god. Structurally, the position of freedom was thus the same: "The realm of freedom really begins only where labour determined by necessity and external expediency ends" (Marx, quoted in Harvey 2010, p. 156). This new regime of obligations set its own non-negotiable, pre-contractual terms which were imposed and experienced as necessary and hence inescapable. Being "not by his own consent or agreement" (as Stair put it) they too structured the mentalities and limits of human action non-consensually. Conformity to these was understood as necessary to being itself – to social being and individual subjectivity – while the supervisory capabilities at its disposal ensured its constancy. Both the categories and the forces drawn on thus materialised with an intensity whose compulsions could forcibly move people around the globe, separate families, take young children from their homes or schools into mines and factories, without appearing to enslave them and all in the service of the new god.

Importantly, these compelling forces did not only apply to those who were to suffer most at the hands of the new market mentality. There was a certain equality of compulsion here that is often masked by the inequality of treatment and outcomes that defines capitalism. For as Harvey points out, the capitalists too were "impelled onward by the coercive laws of competition". Like the workers, capitalists could not afford to slack off either; *their* sense of freedom was also defined by overriding and unyielding obligations: "[F]orced to maximize profit come what may under conditions of competition, individual capitalists *have no choice*" (Harvey 2010, pp. 157, 146, emphasis added). In this sense, they conformed to a logic described by Donne in the previous chapter: the more that capital and competitiveness were valorised and pursued, the ever more tightly bound the capitalist was in having to conform to their strictures.

That there was a close connection between the rise of capitalism and religious organisation and belief has been well-documented. Max Weber provided a cogent account of this in *The Protestant Ethic and the Spirit of Capitalism*. In its early development, Weber argued, capitalism "needed labourers who were available for economic exploitation for conscience's sake" and Christian doctrines were able to supply precepts for precisely such ends (Weber 1930, p. 282). Weber quotes the seventeenth-century Presbyterian puritan Richard Baxter to show how, among other things, the deployment of sin and godliness was used in this way to great effect: Baxter

> warns against the employment of 'heavy, flegmatic, sluggish, fleshly, slothful persons' as servants, and recommends preference for godly servants ... [since] 'a truly godly servant will do all your service in obedience to God, as if God Himself had bid him do it'.
> (Ibid., p. 281)

(Weber comments: "It appears here that the interests of God and of the employers are curiously harmonious". And besides, noted a contemporary of Baxter, "God probably allows so many people to remain poor because He knows that they would not be able to withstand the temptations that go with wealth!" (ibid.).)

But if the connection was not new, there was a difference that came with the full dominance of industrial capitalism in the nineteenth century. Religious belief and the capitalist spirit stayed tied together for some time, but the hierarchy of the relation was inverted. Again, as Weber put it, "Today [capitalism] is in the saddle, and hence able to force people to labour without transcendental sanctions" (ibid., p. 282). On the global imperial scale, for example, of the "three C's" that were offered as part of the narrative of justification for the European colonial powers' "scramble for Africa" in the second half of the nineteenth century, it was Commerce that motivated more, and was more profitable, than either Christianity or Civilisation.

In all these respects we see activity occurring at two levels: one subterranean; the other, of substitution, in the ascendancy. In both senses hybrids of obligation and practices of obedience are central to what was happening. (We will look more closely into this idea of hybridity in the next chapter.) But we should note that discourses of rights also did play an important part in this development, one that should not be underrated. Their role was essentially three-fold: first, the doctrine of sovereign right justified the dispossession of lands by force and overlaid this with the imposition of jurisdictional categories and institutions that were at once legitimatory and the agents for legalised theft. This was the case both domestically and in its imperial mode. Second, the principle of sovereign right instituted the protection of private property rights through constitutional and legal means. The close functional connection between these first two aspects of the role of rights is crucial to both of them. As Moyn puts it, "[P]roperty protections remained by far the most persistent and important rights claim in theory and law (including constitutional law) throughout the nineteenth century and modern history" (Moyn 2010, p. 35).

David Graeber, agreeing that the most powerful notion of rights that emerged in this context was that dominated by a property conception, adds, importantly, that this conception refers not primarily to the right to property itself (though of course that was vital), but to the idea that any and all rights were *themselves* the property of individuals. They belonged to them as of right and this had two significant implications: that others had obligations to respect these rights and that they could only be taken away with the consent of the rights holder. With respect to this latter point, one right in particular was crucial: the right of the labourer to sell his labour power. If such "free labour" was an improvement on that which preceded it, like slave or serf labour, this new freedom had, however, the most paradoxical of

Shifting priorities   53

qualities: "Those who have argued that we are the natural owners of our rights and liberties have been mainly interested in asserting that we should be free to give them away, or even to sell them" (Graeber 2012, p. 206). In other words, the greatest proponents of freeing labour from the shackles of former constraints were also those who knew it could immediately be brought into a different domain of compulsion *and* that this would serve best the interests of those who "bought" the labour, not those who sold it. As Adam Smith, for example, had observed, irrespective of the moral problems with slavery, "the work done by freemen comes cheaper in the end than that performed by slaves" (Smith 1976, p. 99).

Analogously to Simmel's point earlier about the paradoxical structure of authority, in economic terms only if people were free could they *sell* their labour and in doing so voluntarily submit to the authority of the market. If people consented to this in return for money (in the form of wages) and if they sold it for less than it was worth, the voluntary aspect established by the law of contract operated to legitimate the arrangement. Inevitably, under capitalism the wage the workers received was not equivalent to the value of what they produced and surplus value was made from this as profit which did not belong to the producers. But because this had been freely established *and* because all property rights had to be respected, *everyone* (including workers) had legal obligations to respect this property, no matter how exploitatively it had been gained nor how unequally it was now distributed. This was essentially the Stockholm syndrome of political economy and it was essential to the structuring of the new market society. Its – enduring – success relied on the commodification of labour despite the fact that, as Karl Polanyi pointed out, labour was not a commodity in anything other than a purely fictional sense:

> Labor is only another name for a human activity which goes with life itself ... it cannot be shoved about, used indiscriminately, or even left unused, without affecting also the human individual who happens to be the bearer of this peculiar commodity.
> (Polanyi 1957, pp. 72–73)

And yet in so far as it succeeded in being instituted in this way, this was precisely the constitutive and disciplining effect on the labourer.

Here therefore was another and different form of the asymmetry between rights and obligations, this time in the economic realm. Its relation to the political and particularly the legal realm was inextricable. Smith's early insight into this state of affairs was honest, if nothing else:

> Civil government, so far as it is instituted for the security of property, is in reality instituted for the defence of the rich against the poor, or of those who have some property against those who have none at all.
>
> (Smith 1976, p. 715)

If the seventeenth-century conflicts had been fought around the king's power and restraints upon it, then by the nineteenth century the focus had changed. As Polanyi argued, now "industrial property was to be protected and not against the Crown but against the people". Writing of the United States, this meant that "[i]n spite of universal suffrage, American voters were powerless against owners" (Polanyi 1957, pp. 225–226).

So while equality before the law had emerged in contract law to replace the status conceptions that had prevailed before it (to use Maine's formulation), this putative liberation not only occurred unevenly historically and geographically. It took place under two conditions that relied on the prevalence of obligations and practices of obedience over which those subject to them had no control. The first was the *form* of relations of production and exchange which appeared, as we have seen, as non-negotiable obligations to act according to the norms of the new market economy. The legal imprimatur given to this will be taken up in a contemporary setting in Chapter 5. The second was that while obligations had gone "underground" in the dominant accounts of rights that emphasised "free labour" and the decline of status-based regulation, the organisation of social life for the vast majority of people was still predominantly and explicitly organised around obligation-based practices. The costs of this mode of production were largely externalised (as the economists say), meaning that those who created the costs and harms were not responsible for them; instead, the costs were "socialised", a rather euphemistic term for a deeply anti-social situation whereby the effects of externalised costs were borne by those who were least responsible for creating them and who often lacked the resources to redress them. In such a situation, reliance on the fulfilment of obligations – from family and kinship ties to informal workplace relations – was essential to maintaining some kind of tolerable life in the face of harsh conditions imposed by others according to non-negotiable forms of value.

What did not happen, and with one exception has not happened, even at the theoretical level, was the coming forth of any promise of equivalence between rights and obligations (in the sense described by Kant's ideal of autonomy) with respect to the operation of the economy. No conservative or liberal theory in political economy ever promised some notion of equivalence with respect to those who create wealth (all those involved in the production of value) and those who receive wealth or profit from it. The exception to this were socialist doctrines which from the nineteenth century came to play an increasing role in resisting inequalities both in public, governmental spheres and in the realm of privately owned production.

Hence we come to the third role of rights, which was of a different order and complexion. These comprised the increasingly insistent demands against the established order to alleviate the brutalities of the divine economy in action: the rights of children not to be forced into work, the rights of workers to form trade unions, the rights of people to a maximum length of working day, and so on. Each of these was won only in the face of their initial repulsion by prevailing interests, and thus required resistance against these interests and the organised violence of the state which supplied the force behind the law. Yet, on one view, these victories, important as they were, were largely fought and won *within* the structuring categories of the market system: property and labour as commodities to be bought and sold and the private law categories of obligations and property that rested on this, bolstered by the sovereign state that would define and enforce them as legal entitlements.

Nonetheless, these legal and economic conditions contained within them reservoirs of "socialised" obligation which stood outside the formal legalities of commodified labour and its exploitation. But these reservoirs provided resources in two very different ways. On the one hand, they were, as we have just noted, deliberately deployed and relied on as ways of responding to the externalised costs of the market so that responsibilities for social welfare were borne by communities on a non-market basis. As part of this, a whole range of labour practices was treated as *non*-commodifiable, most significantly domestic labour. Almost exclusively the activity of women and girls, this "resource" was drawn on as *literally* free labour. The existence of individual rights as equal entitlements did not play a role there, while obligations and practices of obedience clearly did. This was again the domain of the passive citizen, of those who had many obligations but few rights, and John Donne's line would again have been entirely appropriate to it:

"[T]herefore because you have been so particularly taught your particular duties, therefore perform them, therefore practise them".

On the other hand, aspects of these same reservoirs of solidarity could be drawn on to challenge existing distributions of power. Traces of this could found in various antecedents and are memorably described in one form by EP Thompson in his work on the "moral economy" of the English crowd in the eighteenth century. Revisiting what had been termed by those in power disorderly riots over access to affordable food, Thompson showed how these collective actions involved a claim to legitimacy that was central to the actors' self-understanding. People, wrote Thompson, acted according to "the belief that they were defending traditional rights or customs; and in general, that they were supported by the wider consensus of the community" (Thompson 1971, p. 78). These activities also referred to a "consistent traditional view of social norms, and obligations, and of the proper economic functions of several parties within the community which, taken together, constitute the moral economy of the poor". In claiming such legitimacy, they invoked "definite and passionately held notions of the common weal" (ibid., p. 79) rather than the chaotic individualism associated with either looters or the newly emerging entrepreneurial middlemen. Rights claims thus played a role in legitimising resistance, although even here obligation played a foundational role. For in their outrage – but not their outrages – the poor, as Thompson puts it, were demanding a better response to this fundamental, enduring, and ultimately most humane of questions: "What ought to be men's *reciprocal* duties?" (ibid., p. 91, emphasis added).

In broad terms it is these two modes of obligation – of exploitation and of solidarity – that will be taken up in Chapters 5 and 6. For now, let us draw together what we have covered by noting that the idea that rights and obligations are correlative is, as we saw in Chapter 1, not a necessary idea, but a contingent one, one that comes about fully only in Western modernity. With the invention of rights certain forms of obligation moved into positions of correlativity: if someone had a right, then it *meant* that someone else had an obligation. Obligations were drawn into the service of rights and their protection. But this did not mean that rights and obligations were distributed evenly throughout the populace. As we have seen, the development of modernity relied on their not being so. Moreover, many kinds of obligations remained external to the formal realm of rights and obligations. They still do. Obligations associated with families, kinship, friendship, religions, and so on, all continued as persistent enablers of social relationships, civic order, and economic development, even if in the latter respect they were relied on to "socialise" the costs capitalism engendered. And yet this situation has been consistently underplayed in contemporary legal analyses which focus on the expansion and meaning of rights and neglect the way rights have relied on the persistence, prevalence, and widespread reach of obligations throughout society.

In all this, the existence of mechanisms of what Michel Foucault called "disciplinary power" – forms of power which were not reducible to juridical or sovereign power – played an important role in organising and regulating many of these practices. But we should be wary of underemphasising the continued role of juridical power in this. Foucault claimed that "[w]e have entered a phase of juridical regression in comparison with the seventeenth century societies we are acquainted with" (Foucault 1990, p. 144). But this account would not reckon adequately with the ways in which juridical *aggression* was also key to understanding developments since that period. The idea that people were increasingly "governed through their freedoms", as Foucault's account of governmentality suggested, may have been true in some respects for some people. But more people were governed through their unfreedoms. And law, the subjectivities it set in place, and the obligations and practices of obedience it enforced remained central to this.

4 The ecology of obligations
Situating the legal bond

To understand the specific work legal obligations do in our "age of rights" we need to situate the analysis within the forms and forces of contemporary capitalist society more broadly. I use the notion of an ecology of obligations to do so. In this chapter we will first consider the particular characteristics of legal obligations and what they contribute to the ecology of obligations. We will then seek to understand how legal obligations and practices of obedience combine in modern societies, including in the maintenance of extensive inequalities even where political equality has emerged as a dominant principle. To do this, we will examine the significance of what are described here as hybrids of obligation and obedience. What we will see is how a structure similar to Stair's three-fold account of obedience, freedom, and engagement continues to be central to understanding the ongoing subterranean power of obligations, even in an "age of rights". But given how obligation-obedience hybrids reconfigure the meaning of freedom and engagement, that structure will also need to be supplemented.

In the following section I will explain how the specificity of legal obligations has three characteristics salient to our analysis: they operate between legal persons; they can be turned into things; and they have a distinct mode of enforcement. Before turning to these, however, I want to look briefly at the idea of obligation as a *legal bond* and identify some of its key components. The binding feature of legal obligations requires addressing their normative quality, but it is worth emphasising that the analysis here is not concerned with addressing the question as to whether or not law is morally binding, a question that is discussed in much conventional work. The focus here is instead on the sociological conditions within which legal obligations do their binding work.

Obligations in law

The vinculum iuris

We can begin by analysing more closely the internal structure of an obligation in law. Recall then the definition in Roman Law noted in the Introduction, from Justinian's *Institutes*: "An obligation is a bond of law, by which we are tied down to the necessity of making some performance, according to the laws of the state". (*Obligatio est iuris vinculum, quo necessitate adstringimur alicuius solvendae rei, secundum nostrae civitatis iura*.) Let us break this down.

The original *vinculum* of the "vinculum iuris" comes from *vincire*, to bind. As Peter Birks explains: "A *vinculum* is anything with which binding is done. Hence a fetter, bond, chain or rope" (Birks 2014, p. 3). *Adstringere* too denotes binding: "'to tie up tightly', 'to confine with bonds'" (ibid.). The mental image of the material bond is portrayed vividly in Birks's account:

> An obligation is a rope ... by which we are tied ... Dwell on that image. Here I am with a rope around my neck. We must allow for the other end of the rope. You are holding that. I am under an obligation to you: the picture is of this rope between us, and you in control; the rope is around my neck but in your hand.
> (Birks, ibid., ellipses in original)

This picture also registers something of the flexibility – or constrained movement – of the obligation relationship that is not captured by other images commonly used in describing an obligation. Bentham, for example, also describes as a "fictitious entity" the "material image" of obligation as a cord or tie, but adds that the

> emblematic or archetypal image is that of a man lying down, with a heavy body pressing on him, to wit in such sort as either to prevent him acting at all or so ordering matters that if he does act it cannot be in any other direction or manner than of the manner or direction requisite.
> (Bentham, quoted in Hart 1982, p. 131).

And so with this "primitive situation of the image", adds Hart, we can explain its extension to associated expressions such as "a man being '*under* an obligation' (like a weight) or '*bearing* an obligation', or 'being *relieved* of an obligation'" (ibid., emphases in original). But these formulations lack something which the ancient image captures, the way in which the obligation follows the debtor around as they move, and they downplay the specific nature of the power differential in the relationship. Zimmermann describes this well:

> [T]he concept of an obligation, in the minds of laymen as well as [Roman] lawyers, seems to have retained the connotation of some sort of invisible rope around the neck of the debtor, tying a specific debtor to a particular creditor. The obligation thus gave rise to an intensely personal relationship.
>
> (Zimmermann 1996, p. 5)

A central quality of the obligation is thus portrayed in this image of the person being bound to another by a rope or chain. But the parties are neither equally bound nor bound equally. As AH Campbell puts it, "The chain does not, as the hasty beginner is apt to say, bind the debtor and creditor; it binds the debtor, but the creditor's end lies freely in his hands to use or not as he pleases" (Campbell 1954, p. 31). An obligation is thus a constraint on only one of the parties; the other is entirely free to act as they choose unless they are themselves bound by another obligation.

Birks's careful reading finds something else in Justinian's definition of obligation. That definition, we have noted, says that obligation is a legal bond that ties us "to the necessity" of some performance. The curious thing about this formulation, says Birks, is that "we are tied by two things at once. We are tied by the rope of law, and we are tied by the necessity of acting" (Birks 2014, p. 4). This doubling is crucial to understanding the structure of obligation and the difference it makes in the world. It identifies what it means for there to be a *legal* bond that compels action as necessary. How so? Here is Birks's gloss: the double tie is

> a consequence of having in the one sentence the metaphorical force of the rope *and* the real compulsion of the law itself. The translation [into English] makes the transition from metaphor to reality by saying that we are tied down (by the rope) to the necessity of performing.
>
> (ibid., emphasis added)

Thus an alternative translation of Justinian's definition would be: "[A]n imaginary rope of legal forces whose effect is to compel us to make some performance..." (ibid.). If the person holding the rope in their hands is, as we noted, free to act, the other person is subject to that freedom by means of the bond of obligation; *their* actions are constrained, treated as necessary and non-optional.

But this necessity to act, this compulsion, has a distinctive quality because it too involves a kind of freedom. As Bernard Williams notes in the context of his insightful analysis of "necessity" in Ancient Greece, the kind of constraint that being subject to the power of another involves has this peculiar nature:

> When someone is constrained actually to do something, the typical situation is that there is an *imposed choice*: they are given the alternative of doing what is required, or, on the other hand, pain or death or some other outcome less drastic but also undesirable.
> (Williams 1994, p. 153, emphasis added)

To accept the necessity of performing a particular act is still to have that choice: to accept – or not. (As Williams's reading of Aeschylus shows, even in the extremities of necessity, where Agamemnon must kill his daughter to allow the fleet to sail, Agamemnon "puts on the harness of necessity as someone puts on armour ... [He] takes something that is a necessity and makes it his own" (ibid., pp. 133, 136).)

It is the *normative* nature of the legal bond that explains this freedom under conditions of "the necessity of making some performance". The "vinculum iuris" is invisible, but compels nonetheless. And what is required by way of performance of the obligation is prescribed "according to the laws of the state". This signifies that there is a demarcated zone of obligations, institutionalised in law, that differentiates them from other obligations, and that, simply put, the person is legally required to perform these. But in reality the person obligated might not perform them. At the point where action is required – action that is *necessary* according to the law – they may refuse to act in the way the legal obligation sets out, or act negligently so as to breach the obligation. In doing so, they become liable to some sanction. But whether, in fact, a sanction is executed following the breach is another and separate question from the original existence of the obligation itself. As MacCormick puts it:

> [W]hat is constitutive of duty is the imposition of requirements upon persons as holders of roles, positions or offices, not the presence of any specific or direct sanctioning mechanism ... the

sanctioning measures belong to the particular mode of wrongfulness of particular types of breach or neglect of duty; they are not constitutive of the concept of duty.

(MacCormick 2007, p. 113)

What then is the force of compulsion *internal* to the legal bond? It is precisely that force which prescribes necessity according to the laws of the state. It is analogous to Kant's account of moral obligation: "Obligation is *the necessity of a free action* under a categorical imperative of reason" (Kant 1996, p. 48, emphasis added). This compulsion is, as Birks put it, real: it is necessary to act in a particular way to carry out the obligation. But that compulsion is not the sanction itself. Someone can properly fulfil their legal obligations, for example, aware that they are required, indeed compelled, to do so by the law without any sanction ever being invoked or required or even given consideration by the person obligated. The sanction is not what constitutes the legal bond in the first place.

Obligations in law then are legal ties between persons that describe what actions, in law, are required or necessary to be performed by the one bound by them. These actions are what we call obligatory. Even so, the *actual* actions of the person bound may not conform to what is required. In choosing not to, or in failing to perform the necessary action, they do not, however, negate the existence of the obligation. There is a difference between the freedom not to fulfil an obligation and the freedom to determine whether or not the obligation exists. The latter is prescribed by law and the person obligated is still bound by that obligation even if, in fact, they do not perform it. The importance of emphasising this point will become clear later in this chapter when we look more closely at the existence of obligation-obedience hybrids in which it is precisely that freedom of action that is co-opted by other (non-legal) social practices and mechanisms.

Persons in law

The next feature of the obligation is not explained in Justinian's definition but is implicit in it. Who is the "we" which the legal bond binds in the phrase "by which *we* are tied down"? If, as Zimmermann observed, the obligation originally involved an "intensely personal relationship", what is that "person" like? The straightforward answer to this is "a legal person": legal obligations operate between "legal persons". As such the categories of actors to which they attach is far greater than just human beings. Legal obligations attach to corporations, banks, universities, and so on. Such institutionalised inventiveness means that the scope of obligations in law is far wider than is conceivable, for example, in conventional moral thinking since legal persons are, importantly, not the same as human persons. Although human beings are also normally recognised as legal persons, some may not be (as in some versions of legalised slavery) and many legal persons may not be humans at all, as is the case, for example, with limited liability corporations which separate the legal personality of the corporation from the identity of its human members (even if there is only one of them). Again, we may helpfully turn to MacCormick: "[T]he most basic position or role known to law is that of the legal subject [or person], namely that of a being whose conduct the law regulates". It is thus to such (legal) beings or persons that obligations attach, making a legal obligation "that which one is categorically required to do or refrain from doing *as occupant* of some position or role" (MacCormick 1990, pp. 364–365, emphasis added).

This observation has important implications since it indicates that "role obligation" is the archetypal form of obligations in law and because it will help explain how these have influence far beyond the strictly legal realm of positive law. On the one hand, obligations attach to the role, for example, of public officials, such as judges or government officers, of company directors and trustees, of employers and employees, landlords and tenants, of professionals such as accountants or teachers or lawyers. It is to the different facets and forms of legal roles that obligations and powers or capacities are attached. But obligations are not just a link or bond between legal persons. What is true generally in sociological terms is equally true in law: "[E]very bond implies a broad conception of the person tied by it" (Goffman 1968, p. 160). The requirements contained in legal obligations are therefore also "partly definitive or constitutive of the position, role or office or annexed to the powers thereof" (MacCormick 1990, p. 369). This may be most obvious in cases of official roles – the office of a judge, for example, is a purely institutional creation; it gains its existence and definition through a legally defined role. Likewise, the legal bonds that attach to corporations are part of what constitutes their existence as legal persons ab initio. There is, in other words, a co-originality of identity and obligations in legally defined roles: to have the requirements to act or refrain from acting set out in legal obligations is partly just what it means to be such a person in law.

On the other hand, since any single human individual may, and usually will, occupy multiple legal roles, being an *occupant* of these will contribute more or less directly to the way in which that person lives their life. This is true in terms of public or economic roles – as an employee or tenant, say – as well as in locations traditionally seen as private. For role obligations also attach to individual persons in their various "private" and intimate relations too, such as the legal obligations attached to spouses, parents, guardians, and so on. Legal obligations may not entirely define a role in its most general sense – the legal obligations of parents do not exhaust the obligations of parents, for example – but in so far as legal obligations are ascribed to the *role*, in law, of parents, they partly do define what it means to be a parent. In this way legal obligations, in so far as they apply to people as occupants of different legal roles or positions, are constitutive not just with respect to their *legal* ties, but inevitably also with respect to their social relationships more generally as they stabilise expectations and set opportunities and limitations.

This has one further but very significant implication. Because a single individual will likely be an occupant of a range of legal roles, and since these roles play a crucial part in organising the kind of society we live in, then in so far as this is an unequal society then they too play a part in maintaining such inequalities. For example, a corporation which owns and manages a factory or someone who is an employer or landlord may have reciprocal obligations towards their employees or tenants, but, as we will see in more detail in the following chapter, the former typically have an asymmetrical power to determine the latter's obligations. Consequently, where the operation of legal roles sustains unequal powers and liabilities, then the individual occupants of these roles will find themselves in unequal positions with respect to social relationships and even life chances. The pile of legal selves that sits atop any particular human occupant of them regulates and constitutes what that occupant can or cannot do. Such patterned variations as this produces necessarily upset the ideal of the principle of equality of all before the law, a fact that the voluntary assumption of obligations by individuals will fail to redeem when the broader contextual conditions are taken into account.

The reciprocity between legal personality and obligation highlights that identity and constraint are mutually related through the legal definition of a multiplicity of roles. And as we have just noted, the constitutive link between obligation and identity not only concerns legal institutions and relations, but also plays a crucial role in structuring social relations and expectations more broadly. Moreover, not only is the reach of obligations in law wide, their content is potentially far more detailed and diverse than those involving simply individuals. That is precisely how legal personality and the legal definitions of roles, along with their attendant powers and obligations, are central to spreading the operation of obligations throughout society. But in so far as these have more or less intentionally asymmetric effects, it is also why they are complicit in maintaining inequalities in social relations more generally.

Obligations as things

We now come to the next feature of legal obligations that is central to their contemporary operation and influence. This is one whose inventiveness can also be traced back to Roman Law, and which, at first glance, is perhaps one of the most astonishing features of legal obligations given their "personal" nature as we have just described it. This characteristic is that legal obligations can also be treated as "things", not just as ties between legal persons. In Roman Law, legal obligations were categorised as *res incorporales*, "incorporeal things". The meaning of this abstract formulation is that legal obligations can be "reified", that is, treated as things, and, as things, be transferred to others. One of the most common forms of this is the debt obligation, which can be bought and sold or, to use a different term, commodified. This relies on a second-order transformation of primary obligations – a loan between two people, for example – into tradable assets (rights) through the legalised commodification of liabilities. If this has an ancient legal ancestry, it is also one of the most important aspects of obligations in law in contemporary capitalist societies. This is particularly true where personal and public indebtedness have reached unprecedented levels and where, therefore, debt obligations are central to understanding not only the nature of the economy but its specific impact on society. As David Graeber notes, "Increasingly, corporate profits in America are not derived from commerce or industry at all, but from finance – which means, ultimately from other people's debts. These debts do not happen by accident. To a large degree they are engineered ..." (Graeber 2016, p. 24).

The economic and social function and impact of this role of obligations are difficult to overstate. As the nineteenth-century economist HD Macleod put it: "If we were asked – Who made the discovery which has most deeply affected the fortunes of the human race? We think, after full consideration, we might safely answer – The man who first discovered that debt is a saleable commodity" (quoted in Tolhurst 2006, p. 3). Perhaps the key reason for the importance of this is simply stated: that debt "is someone's asset and income stream, not just someone else's liability" (Blyth 2013, p. 8). In this respect the legal system deploys the modes of constraint and entitlement (obligations and rights) that tie people and their activities in a personal relationship before, in turn, allowing these to be used to generate profits for others through their sale and re-sale.

But the effects are typically asymmetrical, and there is no better example of this than one of the "financial instruments" that lay at the heart of the 2008 financial crash: the "collateralised debt obligation". The "sub-prime" mortgages – loans made by banks to house buyers that were highly risky in terms of their being able to meet repayments – were themselves commodified, packaged together and hyperbolically traded (along with the insurance contracts designed to shore them up) in newly made markets created for this purpose. Trading happened so far removed from the original creditor-debtor relationship which inaugurated them that no-one knew (or bothered) about the original "personal" obligations so long as they could be used to make profit for players in these new markets. As economist John Kay describes it in his analysis of financialisation and its social costs: "The culture of anonymous trading is divorced from economic context, devalues or eliminates personal relationships, and fosters the self-aggrandising self" (Kay 2015, p. 285). When the crash came the asymmetric consequences became even more stark. On the one hand, those with debt obligations in the form of mortgages who were often unable to pay (having been subject to predatory lending practices by financial institutions) still retained the personal obligation to repay; when they defaulted, as was widely seen in the wake of the financial crisis, the rope of law – the *vinculum iuris* – could be firmly pulled on by the banks to remove debtors and their families from their homes. On the other hand, the traders who had profited from the secondary markets lawfully kept their profits while remaining obligation-free with respect to either the original mortgage or the collateral damage caused to the financial system. And if the financiers got away with the money, the politicians in turn acted as a conduit for the continued propagation of asymmetries by bailing out the banks while inflicting harsh austerity conditions on *others*, and especially those who were most vulnerable: the young, the old, the sick, and the insecure for whom social security supports were severely downgraded in many countries. (As Tony Judt remarked of this political rhetoric, there was a time when "being tough consisted of *enduring* pain rather than imposing it on others" (Judt 2010, p. 37, emphasis in original).) Hence the treatment of obligations as things in the form of debts is a vital component in understanding contemporary social relations, and we will return to it in the next chapter.

Law's coercive role

These two characteristics, concerning legal persons and commodification, show how legal obligations play remarkably creative *and* asymmetric functions in modern societies. The third characteristic marks what is common to these, and can be stated quite briefly: that to work as legal obligations they must be enforceable in specific ways. Commonly this means that they are guaranteed and enforceable by a third party, which is usually but not necessarily the state. A range of coercive legal forms, institutions, and actors are involved in this. These will include official court orders (both civil and criminal), law enforcement agencies, regulatory bodies with powers of financial sanction, as well as legally delegated mechanisms made available through debt repossession companies, asset-freezing through banks, and so on. If the sanction is not, as we have just seen, constitutive of the obligation itself, then an array of sanctions and enforcement techniques is, nonetheless, a necessary aspect of their general operation.

Combined with the *priority* of the legal institution's own coercive force vis-à-vis other social norms, the enforceability of legal obligations secures them a presence which other obligations – moral, civic, familial, etc. – lack. This does not mean that legal obligations exist entirely independently. But it does mean that the specific form of enforceability of legal obligations remains a central facet of the organisation of obligations more generally. That is, the force of law can be brought to bear decisively on the broader imposition and distribution of obligations, as well as policing the operation of obligation-obedience "hybrids" – as we will see shortly – as and when required. And in so far as the constitution and operation of legal obligations and roles operate in a capitalist society to maintain differential power relations, law's coercive capacity is necessarily deployed in regulating and sustaining this condition.

The ecology of obligations and obligation-obedience hybrids

Legal obligations function in an environment made up of various institutions and social formations that may be described as constituting the ecology of obligations. Within this ecology, hybrids of obligation and obedience are key to understanding how legal obligations circulate and become effective. In the next chapter I will look in more detail at these through the examples of contract, property, and debt relations. This section sets out the idea of the ecology and the hybrid in more abstract terms.

68 The ecology of obligations

In terms of the natural world an ecology signifies

> the extraordinarily complex and subtle web of organic and non-organic life which is entirely *relational* – so the entities related are constituted by those relationships – and *reflexive*, so that it is impossible to stand outside and observe and manipulate it, either in whole or in part, without affecting it or its other parts, or without being affected by it.
>
> (Curry 2011, p. 8, emphasis in original)

I would like to use these notions of relationality and reflexivity as a way of thinking about how obligations do their work in modern societies. For present purposes then, the "ecology of obligation" should be understood in a double sense.

First, it concerns the main conditions *within* which obligations circulate. Obligations, including legal obligations, do their work through relying on the conditions that make social action and communication in modern societies possible. Among such enabling conditions are very commonplace, if complex, features of modern society that necessarily include natural and technical languages; the myriad instantiations of the division of labour that produce and reproduce dependencies and interdependencies in co-operative and productive practices; material and virtual technologies; economic infrastructures (such as currencies, markets, institutions of finance, circulation, and exchange); and the more or less formally organised groupings in workplaces, institutions, families, bureaucracies, and so on. A list like this is necessarily extensive and always incomplete, but its elements form the conditions within which obligations operate, and without which they cannot operate. Obligations as elementary relations necessarily draw resources from the technologies, materials, expectations, dependencies, disciplines, and coercions made available in these forms. There is, in other words, a wide range of "mediators" of obligations, including many that fall far beyond the vision of conventional and even critical legal analysis (McGee 2014). And while many of these operate within more or less hierarchical, unequal, and exploitative settings, each also involves forms of co-operation and a capacity for individual and collective action that depends on structures of conformity, reliance, and trust. There are of course many more aspects to these institutions than the facilitation of obligations, but obligations, nonetheless, depend on such formations to function.

Second, the "ecology of obligations" concerns the conditions or techniques that obligations *themselves* provide for practices or modes

The ecology of obligations 69

of organisation or regulation. Obligations establish one form of the ties that hold together commitments through constraints. These are central to social practices as varied as friendships, intimate relationships, and the formally institutionalised obligations of office or the market. The ecological contribution provided *by* obligations relies on their capacity to bind: they provide specific modes of communication and action that are or at least claim to be non-optional – necessary, in the normative sense we described earlier. They bind people to each other or to institutions or expectations in a way that entitlements (or rights) do not, because their primary mode of existence is connective and constraining.

It will be clear already that these two senses of the ecology of obligation are interconnected. Obligations rely for their operation on social and economic conditions, structures, and expectations that rely in turn on obligations to function. This is exactly why the features of relationality and reflexivity in natural ecologies are apt in describing how obligations do their work: obligations depend upon but also help constitute social formations in such a way that they are indissociable from the "complex web" within which they operate and to which they contribute. It is also why they retain, as we noted in earlier chapters, a priority even as rights hold the dominant position in general discourse.

In this ecology, hybrids of obligation and obedience are an essential part of how legal obligations work. A hybrid here refers to the combination of the normative aspect made available through legal obligations with factual or empirical practices of obedience secured by other, non-legal, means. Practices of obedience refer then to ways of organising or governing activities and behaviour in which conformity is already essentially guaranteed. If legal obligations, as normative, retain an element of freedom, practices of obedience co-opt that freedom through non-legal techniques. These techniques limit, organise, shape, and structure the space and meaning of freedom and do so in mostly non-consensual ways. Instead, their operation tends to be similar to that of obediential obligations as Stair described: they bind actors "not by [their] own consent or engagement". Such hybrids as we are concerned with here may exist in ways that *pre*-structure the operation of legal obligations or flow *from* the creation of legal obligations. In both places it is significant that legal rights play only a secondary or supportive role and, instead, the primacy of obligation is secured through the hybrid form. And whereas legal rights and obligations might be explicitly amenable to discourses of legal or political contestation and legitimation, hybrids of obligation and obedience typically do their work externally to such discourses.

In this sense they are similar but have a different emphasis to Michel Foucault's notion of "the norm". This "new law", as he describes its emergence in modernity in his path-breaking work *Discipline and Punish*, is "a mixture of legality and nature" combining "the legal register of justice and the extra-legal register of discipline" (Foucault 1995, pp. 304, 301). The meaning of the hybrid form here places more emphasis on the fact that law itself plays crucial constitutive and disciplinary functions. This is not least the case with respect to the subject positions that are made available through legal personality which define, organise, and constitute how occupants of a role must be and act, with little or no input from the occupants themselves. This begins as soon as we arrive in the world: a compulsory birth certificate legally defines us in terms of gender, name, and so on, and stays with us, literally, as a certifying marker to be transferred to other documents and categories as we pass through officialdom – nationality, citizenship, passport, etc. – almost all aspects of the functioning of which are equally non-consensual. Rather than law being understood as an institutional form of justice and right which subjects freely use and sovereign power guarantees, law's obligatory and power-conferring (Hart 1961) functions construct the kinds of normative freedom and unfreedom available to legal (and thus human) persons. Law, in other words, is itself a productive form of discipline in which legal categories and roles constitutively structure and define what count as freedoms and responsibilities, and in this sense legal subjects are not at liberty to individually determine their own capacities or the terms on which they are engaged.

This form in turn is inseparable from the disciplinary determinations provided by the wider environment, such as those found in the economic or technological infrastructure of a society. These non-legal techniques and modes of operation further define and constrain the options that legal actors have. In order to be effective, in other words, laws and their binding quality have a necessary relationship with practices of obedience so that their operation is guaranteed over time. It is this relationship we can think of as being hybrid. The legal norm operates as something of a gateway through which other more demanding and less consensual forms of obedience are set to work. For example, what may appear as (or in fact be) an initial consent – signing a mortgage agreement, for example – requires certain non-optional assumptions to be first put in place about the "person" who is capable of making this legal agreement. Subsequently, the agreement constitutes and situates actors within other domains of *non-consensual* conformities, for instance, the exposure to interest rate or market fluctuations. There are no longer *individual* decisions to be made with respect to the

The ecology of obligations   71

overall operation of these; instead, a whole range of obedience practices is set to work in binding people's behaviour.

In this sense, the non-consensual conformities made available through practices of obedience cannot be disassociated from the legal form. They must be seen as already acting together. In this respect there is nothing especially new about them: the hybrid form is central to the operation, circulation, and achievement of legal obligations in the ecological environment generally. Whether these work for good or bad effects, or for whom they are good or bad, is a separate and no doubt contestable issue. In the next chapter we will consider how hybrids set the possibilities of obligatory action in asymmetric ways, depending on the particular domain in which they are operating. In the final chapter we will see how they are also important for ends that aid community flourishing. As we noted in the Introduction, context matters.

But to appreciate why and how these hybrids are so potent, we may refer to an insight from Thomas Hobbes about obedience to law. Writing of the authority of the sovereign over its subjects (and, we may note in passing, giving a wonderful description of *vincula iuris*) Hobbes observes that the sovereign establishes

> Artificiall Chains, called Civill Lawes, which [men] themselves, by mutual covenants, have fastened at one end to the lips of that Man, or Assembly, to whom they have given the Soveraigne Power; and at the other end to their own Ears. These Bonds in their own nature but weak, may nevertheless be made to hold, by the danger, though not by the difficulty of breaking them.
> (Hobbes 1996, p. 147)

Our interest is in the last part of this observation. Leaving aside the constitutive function of legal personality, Hobbes sees law as a normative order that provides for the freedom of people to *obey* the law that is at exactly the same time a freedom to *break* the law. And, ever the realist, Hobbes observes, breaking the law is *not* difficult to do. But it may be, and for Hobbes certainly *should* be, dangerous to do so: in order to maintain a secure and peaceful society, sanction or punishment – "the sword" as he calls it – should follow from any breach.

The key point about hybrids of obligation and obedience, however, is that they contain both elements: freedom to obey and disobey an obligation *and* the unfreedom and conformity of practices of obedience whose specific quality lies in the fact that they are *not* easy to break. The legal "gateway" into these might be thought to be rather like a gateway drug: the first step leads to other, stronger material. Like an addictive drug habit, what follows goes far beyond the initial freedom or control of the agent. Once entered, practices of obedience are, unlike legal norms, very *difficult* to break. Of course, the analogy goes only so far. For what these practices of obedience actually do in a society may be beneficial too. Yet at a purely descriptive level, these forms of binding constraint are reciprocally reliant on the legal form to structure and induce entry. And while legal obligations are necessary to institute or inaugurate entry into these practices, they remain in one sense easy to breach. But this fact explains neither the full extent of the operation of the law nor the necessities or constraints that maintain its particular field of operation.

Such hybrids are, I suggest, key to law's operations; they do, we might say, much of the unseen but heavy lifting of law in modern society. Yet they tend to be unaccounted for in most jurisprudential analyses. What this suggests is that the specific types of hybrids of obligation and obedience are so woven into our social and mental fabrics that seeing them as integral to legal analysis is a demanding task even theoretically. Gaining an understanding of the operation of hybrids of obligation and obedience throws up different and challenging types of question – particularly about autonomy and freedom – that appear awkward or even hard to register within our current legal thinking. But shifting our attention to them and away from a dominant rights perspective allows us to understand better the work they do within the ecology of obligations.

To see the significance of these hybrids in practice I will focus in the next chapter on three areas of legal activity: work contracts, property, and debt. These are selected primarily because of their importance in structuring large parts of people's lives, namely, in their work and workplaces, their involvement in property relations, and their opportunities as influenced by contemporary economic conditions.

5 Hybrids in action
Three contemporary legal formations

Working obligations

By way of an introductory example of the hybrid form, recall something mentioned at the end of Chapter 3, the contract for work, and consider what it involves, and what it assumes and entails. As we noted earlier, at one level such a contract is established, in law, by the freely made agreement between two formally equal parties. But what does this *already* assume before the contract is entered into? It assumes that the labour power of the worker *can* be commodified and bought and sold as such. It also assumes that, as a *commodity*, its price will ultimately be determined not by the parties themselves but by the wider economic conditions: the price of labour is, in other words, generally that which the market can bear. With respect to the totality of these conditions, the individual worker – and even the employer – has no freedom or determining capacity. Furthermore, in terms of the voluntary "engagement" (to use Stair's term) the worker will have little or, more usually, no input into setting the terms of the contract they do in fact agree to, since these are either determined entirely by the employer or subject to terms imposed on them by statute and private law doctrines (Dukes 2019, p. 414). The latter may also include obligations imposed on the employer for the benefit of the worker, addressing conditions as varied as statutory holidays, minimum wage and provision for sick pay, principles of non-discrimination, or employer's liability for employee negligence in the course of employment. Workers' rights in the contract for work can thus be understood to depend for their protection upon a range of further obligations being met. Such obligations – often non-negotiable by the contracting parties themselves – are far more and varied than the rights they protect.

There are at least two dimensions subsequent to entry into the workplace which rely on the hybrid form. First, the formal freedom of the juridical realm protected in theory by equal rights sees the worker immediately inserted into new conditions that now discipline the worker in an obligatory manner. That is, the contract for work establishes certain obligations on workers, but these (if they are stated at all) are ordinarily couched in very broad terms referring to as yet unenumerated obligatory actions to be performed in accordance with managerial directives, such as the performance of duties specified on an ongoing basis by line-managers. In this way, the contract operates like a legal gateway through which, once entered, the worker becomes subjected to changeable workplace obligations that in fact govern almost all aspects of the material and intellectual labouring conditions in which their daily routine consists. These typically include anything from when and how long to take breaks to the varied modes of monitoring workers' behaviour, from imposed target-setting and performance reviews to sanctioning infractions through internal disciplinary mechanisms. With respect to the last of these, as Atiyah points out in his description of the shrinking arena of freedom and consent in the context of contract law, "[t]he employees of a company may indeed have contractual relations with the company itself, but in pursuit of the company's own objectives, it is *the command structure of the company* which settles disputes, not the norms of contract law" (Atiyah 1979, p. 723, emphasis added). This internal "command structure" is paramount, since it is within *this* that the ongoing determination of further workplace obligations takes place. These too are far more and varied than the original contractual obligations agreed to for they include not only obligations but hybrids of obligation and obedience. Collins et al. sum up the general situation in these terms: "[T]he employer acquires the right to direct and manage employees, and employees are obliged to obey those instructions". This amounts to "complete control over the workplace in every respect ... [it] confer[s] discretionary power on the employer to vary the employee's performance obligations" (Collins et al. 2019, pp. 5–6).

The second dimension of hybridity can be identified from the observation that workplace relations are not always – indeed, in large workplaces, more often they are not – straightforwardly conducted through direct employer/employee exchanges. Rather, forms of management *technique* are central to how workplace relations and activities are shaped through hybrids of obligation and obedience that "direct and manage" workers. Such techniques can take varied forms, in part depending on the specific nature and structure of the workplace itself. But there will often be generic forms that are successfully deployed across many different kinds of workplace. Perhaps most apposite to the current context of hybrids are those that organise practices of obedience through "management by objectives". This has the peculiar structure whereby workers' obedience is secured not directly through the performance of legal obligations, but by other, indirect means. That is, the practice of obedience is ensured by the internalisation of objectives such that striving to attain goals becomes the mode of producing obedient behaviour.

Alain Supiot provides an excellent example of this from a 1950s management textbook:

> What the business enterprise needs is a principle of management that will give full scope to individual strength and responsibility ... Management by objectives and self-control makes the interest of the enterprise the aim of every manager. In place of control from the outside, it substitutes the *stricter, more exacting, and more effective* control from the inside. It motivates managers to action, not because someone tells them to do something or talks them into doing it, but because *the objective task demands it*. They act not because somebody wants them to but because they themselves decide that they have to – they act, in other words, as free men and women.
>
> (P Drucker, quoted in Supiot 2018, p. 146, emphases added)

That last observation initially appears to replicate the sense of freedom in the "necessity to perform" identified earlier in the account of legal obligation. But it is not, and the difference is crucial. While legal obligation – in this instance the contract of work – is the gateway through which individuals as employees enter this new realm in return for a wage, "necessary performance" here is, by contrast, established through techniques of management that secure conformity in a different mode. Such forms of control are "stricter, more exacting" precisely because they set standards of correct behaviour by managerial objectives internalised *as* appropriate to "freely acting" subjects, but only in so far as they are first of all produced as *obedient* subjects.

Contemporary manifestations of this abound. For example, the widespread use of targets set by "performance indicators" are increasingly common in workplaces – including universities – and can be seen as exemplars of what Supiot (2018) calls more generally a regime of "governance by numbers". According to these, the organisation and evaluation of "human resources" (as workers are now commonly referred to) is carried out through techniques of quantification that combine objective-setting with modes of inculcated "self-control" to compel specific kinds of "free" action. But they do so not with respect to the legal obligation, but because the "objective task" of the numerical indicators demands it. The increasing use of "league tables" across many work sectors is exemplary in this regard. Having been associated traditionally with sports competitions, these have now become a disciplinary technique embedded throughout nearly all institutional forms – from pre-schools to universities, from internet "hits" to academic citation indices. Of course, such rankings not only reflect a triumph of form over content – in that they must in most cases reduce complex practices to numbers in order that comparison can take place – but they track, because they depend upon and respond to, an intensification of commodification across institutions. The implicit obligation to rise up the league table (after all, who would "freely choose" to drop *down* the table?) thus provides a new form of obligatory conduct for employees *and* institutions themselves in competition with others. Such compulsion relies then on techniques of quantification and the valorisation and internalisation of competitive mind-sets which are often alien and insensitive to the multifaceted nature and internal values of particular activities or practices. Nowhere is this most obviously problematic than in the simple observation that by identifying "winners", league tables inevitably produce many more "losers". In sports this may well be painful for supporters. When they apply to pre-schools and universities as much as to sales of consumer goods, competitive struggles which produce losers may be thought to be more troubling.

With rare exceptions, these managerial dynamics are not reviewable by reference to legal norms. In a sense, that is understandable. Yet what this signifies is that the formation of legal obligations is used simultaneously to *establish* the space for practices of obedience, and then to withdraw from that space leaving the latter almost entirely to the discretion of the employer or managerial technique. *But*, and this is why the hybrid form remains important, the legal obligation remains a reference point that can operate both as a justification for adjusting obligations and as a constant warning that termination may ensue at any time. The overall effect of this double bind is to make "employment more of an autocratic governance mechanism than a contractual bargain" since "through threats of termination [the contract of employment] can always be altered unilaterally in the interests of the employer" (Collins et al. 2019, p. 6).

That the freedom of the worker *is* at some point referred back to is visible in a final exemplary situation. Here workers (and would-be workers) are themselves increasingly made to take responsibility for economic conditions over which they have no say or impact.

Symptoms of this recent phenomenon are to be found in contemporary discourses of responsibilisation, resilience, and mindfulness. Here, the effects of structural economic conditions are supposed to be ameliorated by the obligatory internalisation of responsibility and self-care. Such discourses instilling "appropriate attitudes" not only have proliferated and become dominant within workplaces but are increasingly inaugurated and ingrained as mentalities in places of formative education. That these attitudes should be seen as "mindful" rather than as a preparation for accepting dependency, insecurity, and precarity with respect to conditions over which they have no control is quite an achievement. In this sense, obliging individuals to take responsibility in these ways marks the practical efficacy and formative reach of the hybrid form in co-opting and re-describing individual freedom with respect to working conditions.

The modern, large workplace cannot be properly understood, even in its legal dimensions, without paying attention to the hybrids of obligation and obedience which operate to determine the working conditions of employees and the unequal relations they engender and reproduce. There is, in other words, a "complex web" of legal and non-legal obligations and practices of obedience whose elements are reflexively related and which locate working lives within this part of the ecology of obligations. The legal and personal "freedoms" they presuppose and rely on are in this way co-opted within relations of dependency that simultaneously undermine the credibility of these as freedoms.

Property conditions

There is a deeper context to these observations that we must now turn to. This deals with the economic conditions which provide an essential part of the ecology of obligations in a capitalist economy and which also themselves rely on often unarticulated hybrids. The general circumstances can be outlined reasonably clearly; here is Adam Smith in his lectures to the Jurisprudence class at the University of Glasgow in the 1760s:

> The labour and time of the poor is in civilised countries sacrificed to the maintaining of the rich in ease and luxury. The landlord is maintained in idleness and luxury by the labour of his tenents [sic], who cultivate the land for him as well as for themselves. The moneyd man is supported by his exactions from the industrious merchant and the needy who are obliged to support him in ease by a return for the use of his money.
>
> (Smith 1978, p. 340)

78 Hybrids in action

Essentially unchanged since Smith's day, our questions in this section will address what explains this situation, how is it maintained, and what the role of law is in it.

Smith himself of course thought that free markets could offer expression to natural liberty, but he identified a source of compulsion – economic necessity – that saw the poor obliged to submit to this situation. But implicit in this description is a set of roles and legal categories that not only makes this possible, but also explains how the weaker parties are "obliged to support" the stronger even if the latter are entirely *dependent* on the labouring poor for their "idleness and luxury". This connects us back to another sense of necessity, one that we touched on briefly in Chapter 3. It concerns the problem of the freedom of action in the context of a capitalist society, and the way in which legal institutions are implicated in this. As we saw earlier, a capitalist market depends on the supply of labour and this labour must somehow be *compelled* to work, for a price, and for a price that is evidently less than the value of what it produces: if processes of production are necessarily social, the distribution of profit is not. Let us now explore this further.

Pashukanis identifies an important distinction between the structural *conditions* within which legal persons operate and the characteristics attributed *to* those persons. There is, he writes, a division between

> reified relations (including all economic relations: price level, rate of surplus value, profit rates and so forth) – in other words, the kind of relations in which people have no greater significance than objects – and, on the other hand ... relations where man is defined only by contrast with an object, that is as a subject. The latter exactly describes the legal relation ... At the same time, therefore, that the product of labour becomes a commodity and a bearer of value, man acquires the capacity to be a legal subject and a bearer of rights.
>
> (Pashukanis 2002, pp. 112–113)

On this account, it is the former economic relations that *pre*-structure what are made available as conditions of possibility for the legal person. Or, as he puts it:

> After he has become slavishly dependent on economic relations, which arise behind his back in the shape of the law of value, the economically active subject – now as a legal subject – acquires,

in compensation as it were, a rare gift: a will, juridically constituted, which makes him absolutely free and equal to other owners of commodities like himself.

(ibid., p. 114)

Thus the products of labour and labour itself are commodified and both become the object of legal regulation, the former as property and the latter as freedom to contract. But that the form of value happens "behind the backs" of people signifies that it is not a matter for their legal consent or variation. And yet it binds them, even without these. This is why the idea of Stair's "obediential obligation" is in one sense appropriate here; this form of value is pre-contractual (in Stair's terms), "immediately obliging without any tie upon him by himself". This "law of value" does not exist then as a form of *legal* obligations imposed by the state, such as those one might find in tort law or taxation or criminal law. It has instead an axiomatic quality on which all these further legal obligations depend. Indeed, in a capitalist economy, the state too not only respects this "law of value", but typically sees *itself* bound to uphold it, writing into its constitution the security of property, freedom of labour, formal equality before the law, and so on, that are essential legal protections for the imperatives of this prior law.

While the protection of private property expectations is central to the "law of value", if we understand this only with respect to the security of rights, we miss out much of the varied effects of obligation and the practices of obedience this protection entails. Robert Hale, an early influence in the American Legal Realist movement of the first half of the twentieth century, studied the role of law and in particular property law in ways that help to supplement our analysis on this point. When the state "protects a property right", Hale argues, "[p]assively it is abstaining from interference with the owner when he deals with the thing owned; actively it is forcing the non-owner to desist from handling it, unless the owner consents" (Hale 1923, p. 471). This insight is taken up most starkly when Hale considers the coercive role of the law of property in market and labour practices, detailing how the combination of ownership and coercion is central to securing the subjugation of labour power. People must eat to live, writes Hale, but those who legally own foodstuffs or their means of production are entitled to keep them unless they are offered payment.

There is no law to compel them to part with their food for nothing. Unless, then, the non-owner can produce his own food, the law compels him to starve if he has no wages, and compels him to go without wages unless he obeys the behests of some employer. It is the law that coerces him into wage-work under penalty of starvation.

Property law protects the private interests of owners not simply in the sense of securing non-interference with their property. It is through doing this that, in turn, allows market forces to operate as precisely that: *forces*, generated within the legally organised market and affecting social relations in ways that compel obedience. The private law of property thus helps coerce people into the market or workplace or else they starve from lack of access to necessities of food or the means to produce it. This is the "law-made dilemma", says Hale, "of starvation or obedience" (ibid., p. 473). Given the public role of the state in licensing such coercion, the operation of force in a supposedly "free" market of private property owners should therefore be recognised as a combination of public and private power underpinned by the law of value noted by Pashukanis. Contrary to the view that only planned economies coerce market activities and distributions, "free markets", based on freedom of property in ownership and exchange, rely profoundly on coercion and compulsion (as of course most workers and the unemployed know only too well). Both forms thus require the state to be interventionist. But in addition to such centralised coercion, the "free" market also operates in a decentralised way, and that this is another, if different, form of distributed political sovereignty over people's private lives should likewise be acknowledged. With a remarkable prescience for our own times, Morris Cohen, a contemporary of Hale, concludes:

> [W]e must not overlook the fact that dominion over things is also *imperium* over our fellow beings ... There can be no doubt that our property laws do confer sovereign power on our captains of industry and even more so on our captains of finance.
> (Cohen 1927, p. 13)

That the state and its laws protect property and its compelling, obedience-inducing effects in this manner may seem to suggest they do so with respect to property as something pre-existing its regulation. But this would neglect something of the greatest significance when it comes to property rights in modern capitalist societies. That is, that with respect to some of the major and most powerful forms of property, and the legal persons who own and manipulate them, the law's

Hybrids in action 81

role is *entirely constitutive* in their formation. MacCormick describes this as follows:

> The assets of the population, and especially of its wealthiest citizens, are not just protected by the laws against trespass, theft and the like. They *have no existence at all* apart from the law and the legal regimes in which they are encapsulated (or, as we might say, institutionalized).
> (MacCormick 2008, p. 149, emphasis added)

The complex areas of private law – companies and commercial law, financial law, trusts and equity, and so on – which often seem the driest and most apolitical of doctrinal concerns, provide the legal bedrock for a system of wealth generation and maintenance that requires huge legal, institutional, and regulatory effort to create and sustain. Indeed, the lawyers, accountants, and other intermediaries involved would not be paid the very handsome fees they are, by the highly money-conscious people employing them, if they were merely occasionally greasing the wheels of transactions carried out by the principals themselves. Rather, the incomes of such intermediaries reflect the complex intellectual labour required in the creation and supervision of these wealth-generating legal forms; they are, one might say, an index of these *as* constitutive activities (Pistor 2019, ch. 7). To treat property as a negative liberty right over a pre-existing thing that can be brought to the market overlooks this: there is simply no property to protect without law's extensive regulatory effort to produce it. As Paddy Ireland notes:

> [I]n respect of the intangible rights to receive future revenues (the financial property forms) that lie at the heart of contemporary capitalism ... there is no concrete object of property independent of law to which the rights relate; the very "thing" that is owned is a legal construct ... These property forms are regulation all the way down.
> (Ireland 2011, p. 30)

In a capitalist economy then, states are obliged to provide extensive supports for all these endeavours through enacting legislation, the provision of courts, tribunals, enforcement mechanisms, and so on. To deliberately ignore all such activity may go some way to explaining the common mis-perception (although common to whom?) that the people who gain most from the state's redistributive policies are those who "free-ride" on state handouts in the form of social security and other welfare "benefits". But this is neither empirically correct nor conceptually well-informed. To rectify the mis-perception, we need do no more than ask a simple question: "Who would lose disproportionately if the existing political order collapsed under some form of political revolution?" (MacCormick 2008, p. 149). On the one hand, it is the wealthier and middle classes who have always benefitted most from state provisions, even those of the welfare state (Garland 2016). On the other, it is the most wealthy who get the most benefit from the legal constitution and protection of property. Even the use of tax havens to make assets disappear from the radar of state taxation relies on extensive legal, financial, and regulatory structuring backed up by states. (The losses in tax revenue to governments – estimated to be around USD500 billion annually (TJN 2019) – put the notion of the "benefits cheat" in proper perspective.) But they do so also – and this was precisely Smith's realism – by relying on *others* meeting *their* obligations both in workplaces (where hybrids of obligation and obedience operate in ways we have seen) *and* by paying their taxes to support the provision of infrastructure, education, healthy workers, and so on. Through the complex structures of corporate, trust, and (ironically) taxation laws, wealthy actors and corporations are thereby able to free-ride on the backs of others to become literally "duty free" (Veitch 2018). But such "freedom" is reliant on the power of obligations and their hybrids with respect to the vast majority of the working and tax-paying population.

Within the ecology of obligations, the compelling effects of hybrids of obligation and obedience established through the operation of property and corporate forms are thus essential to maintaining the differentials of power and (increasing) inequalities of wealth both within and across societies in a global capitalist economy. Even if he saw the free market as an expression of natural liberty, Adam Smith's observation about the role of law would, nonetheless, have registered a continuity:

> When ... some have great wealth and others nothing, it is necessary that the arm of authority should be continually stretched forth, and permanent laws or regulations made which may [secure] the property of the rich from the inroads of the poor, who would otherwise continually make incroachments upon it.
>
> (Smith 1978, p. 208)

Before ending this part of the analysis we should observe one final aspect of how the "law of value" operates "behind the backs" of legal and social actors. Earlier we quoted Rousseau's insight that the strong are never strong enough always to be master unless they transform strength into right and obedience into obligation. But what we have seen is that this is a transformation in which the former – strength and obedience – must continue to survive the change: that right and obligation on their own do not work successfully without forming hybrids with strength and obedience. So we can add now a third or supplemental aspect of the transformation Rousseau identified: the transformation of contingency into necessity. With respect to the "law of value" this becomes especially important since the hybrid created reveals that the quality of normativity appears differently from that of legal obligation.

We may understand this facet by considering an analogy with Stanley Milgram's account of obedience to authority. What he calls the "groundwork for obedience" is set through a number of social forms that authority commonly takes, from the family to more or less impersonal institutions. One observation he makes in the context of the former provides a key insight into the hybrid relationship of obligation and obedience. When parents provide moral injunctions to children, writes Milgram, they relay not only the explicit content to be followed – "Don't strike smaller children", to use his example – but simultaneously "a second and implicit, imperative: 'And obey me!'" The child learns, in other words, how to act not only with respect to his or her peers, but with respect to the authority figure itself. This latter aspect, implicit but necessary, is essential in training "the child to comply with authoritative injunctions per se" (Milgram 1974, pp. 135–136). The impact of this is something Milgram describes as crucially formative for practices of obedience to authority in other aspects of later life; namely, that when it comes to authority, "relationship overwhelms content" (Milgram 1992, p. 172). It is this relationship and its second implicit imperative – "Obey me!" – that captures something of the way in which the *law* of value works on social relations and subjects. For the implicit quality of its imperative registers its power: when its injunctions are fully and extensively instituted it is one that no longer needs to be articulated as such. And once "learned", it can be forgotten; it becomes second nature and thus, in Hobbes's terms, all the more "difficult to break". It appears, if indeed it registers at all, not as contingent but as a necessity.

Such imperatives and their compelling effects are, of course, no more "natural" than is the particular form of this law of value itself, which had historically to be inculcated through various forms of disciplining on more or (usually) less willing subjects. To ensure its injunctions were instituted, radical alterations in people's working and social conditions were necessary. This is a training in new necessities that continues today in "developing" countries like Cambodia and Bangladesh as they are drawn into the global market to supply cheap labour for consumer goods throughout the world. So profound are these imposed practices of obedience that one of the key techniques requires establishing as a necessity "modern" notions of time and time-keeping in order to regulate working days in hours and even minutes (Thompson 1993). In this process, a foundational equation of the law of value – that "Time is money", still drummed into reluctant participants everywhere – becomes axiomatic to learning that anything and everything else can be money too. This is the contingency-turned-necessity of the law of value in action. But far from being "natural", this new temporality and its accompanying techniques – factory time, billing time, time-tracking software, and so on – are modernity's inventions, central to a "civilising" mission that formed – and forms – the core obediential practices of "market forces" in capitalist systems.

At a primary level then, this particular form of hybridity – of obligatory norms of the capitalist law of value combined with obediential practices – is instituted through a range of logics and material operations and forces, from commodification of labour markets based on supply and demand, to borrowing and lending rates, exchange rates, price indices, and so on. Property law and constitutional guarantees in turn supplement and fix these through the formation, regularisation, and enforcement of legal rights and obligations in a way that contributes to the operation and impact of hybrids of obedience and obligation. Legal norms in this sense act as the gateway to disciplinary mechanisms which provide operational force to both legal obligations and the norms of the economic law of value. Thus is real work done through the ecology of obligations within which habits and practices of obedience do their constraining work. And all this is most effectively achieved through the internalisation of mind-sets and rituals that embed obligatory norms as implicitly necessary, as "control from the inside".

To return to Stair's trio – obedience, freedom, and engagement – what we see here is that the freedom and rights "to engage" in market relations are equally situated in the space between two forms of obligation and obedience. On the one hand, freedoms are pre-structured by obligatory norms of the law of value and their expression in legal form, and on the other engagement is co-opted within the disciplinary forms supplied within the ecology of obligations, especially those of the workplace.

Indebtedness

Our third example of hybrids returns us to debt, and specifically to the issue of indebtedness and practices of obedience that accompany it in its wider socio-economic context. The contemporary global situation with respect to indebtedness cannot be grasped by looking at the obligation relationship alone, or even thousands of these as discrete arrangements. A wider view of contextual factors needs to be taken into account in order to fully understand the operation of debt obligations today. For it is in assessing the conditions that underwrite debt, so to speak, that we will get a sense of the role of legal obligations more broadly in our "age of rights". Here again the non-legal aspects of obedience need to be brought into the frame. To do so, let us first get a brief sense of the magnitude of the issue.

Interestingly, over exactly the same period as the discourse of human rights has come to ever greater prominence (Moyn (2010) suggests this period begins only in the 1970s), so too has financial indebtedness. It would be difficult to show any direct correlation – no doubt other things have increased enormously during this time – but it is certainly the case that personal, corporate, and government debt as a percentage of GDP have soared over the last 40 years. The growth in levels of student and consumer debt in the United States and the United Kingdom are but smaller symptoms of a far larger phenomenon, one that Wolfgang Streeck identifies as a shift in the second half of the twentieth century from a tax state to a debt state (Streeck 2014). Thus, in the decade since the financial crisis alone, for example, global debt increased by USD57 trillion, to a figure which now totals (in 2019) almost USD250 trillion (Mckinsey 2015, 2018). Put differently, having increased by a third in the last ten years alone, global debt now stands at more than three times global GDP, its highest ever level in peacetime (Reuters 2017; FT 2019). The rapid economic growth of the world's most populous country has also figured substantially in this since Chinese debt has quadrupled in just the last seven years, largely a result of the housing boom, and its debt-to-GDP ratio now stands at over 300% (Reuters 2019). In turn, the Chinese government owns over USD1.1 trillion of US debt, around one quarter of all that held by foreign governments, and it has engaged in a "Belt and Road Initiative" extending throughout poorer countries and which has been described as "debt trap diplomacy" given its mode of operation. Large-scale indebtedness is, in these and many other ways, central to contemporary international political economy and foreign policy strategies, and the Covid-19 pandemic has exacerbated this. To this saturation of indebtedness should be added the number of people globally in debt bondage and forced labour – identified among modern forms of slavery that disproportionally affect women and girls (UN 2019) – which, while outlawed, comprises a figure that currently reaches into the tens of millions. This includes many millions of children often bound to labour as a result of intergenerational debt transmission.

Debt, as we noted earlier, makes money – for some. But since debt is "a claim on future labour" the more commonly felt effect of a general increase in debt is to limit personal (as well as political) futures. As David Harvey expresses it, "The whole debt structure forms a vast network of social control that curtails basic freedoms" (Harvey 2018, pp. 434–435). Our concern here is to consider briefly the role of and impact on states, and the unequal effects this has on citizens. In essence, what is occurring even in these states where political equality has been achieved is a reorganisation of the priorities of obligation. This takes place in ways that have dynamic and asymmetric consequences since the changing relations between states and markets result in practices of obedience that limit activities for specific economic ends.

Streeck's account makes a number of important observations in this regard. First, he notes how the "rising indebtedness of the rich democracies has for some time been curtailing their effective sovereignty, by subjecting the policies of their governments to the discipline of financial markets" (Streeck 2014, p. 84). This is achieved through the prioritisation of creditors' (or investors') rights ahead of the claims of society. States are not innocent in this regard, however. Rather, this situation is the result of policy decisions in which states – or rather particular interests within states – are necessarily complicit. State involvement is registered by the amount of legal regulation and deregulation that is required to facilitate the ascendancy of profit-producing indebtedness. The effect, even in advanced economies, is significant in terms of circumscribing the future. Writing of the European Union, for example, Streeck argues that

> under the pressure of financial markets and international organizations, [member states] will have tied themselves to market principles in international and constitutional law and will largely have forfeited the possibility of modifying them in the name of social justice. At that point, the liberalization of modern capitalism will have achieved its objective by durably immunizing its markets from discretionary political interferences.
>
> (ibid., p. 91)

In this sense, the modern state has become, says Streeck, a "consolidation state".

The objectives pursued are thus undoubtedly redistributive, and in that respect they have succeeded. But redistribution has essentially been up the way, from the majority of society to the wealthy. This explains in part why the same period of the growth of indebtedness has been marked by an unprecedented rise in inequality: increasing disparities of wealth within countries and globally has resulted in a situation in which the 26 richest people in the world collectively now own more than does half the world's population (Oxfam 2019) Thus even where political equality and equality before the law have been achieved, where "democracy is tamed by markets instead of markets by democracy" there is a change in focus from the primary obligations of states towards their citizens, to one in which their role is principally that of facilitating and servicing debts. Simply stated, this transformation results in, as Streeck puts it, "not a 'duty to protect' [citizens] but a duty to pay [creditors]" (ibid., p. 116). The regulatory authority of states is necessary to achieve this since, as we saw earlier, this authority is essential in defining and protecting property. But once states themselves become thoroughly integrated within international financial institutions which prioritise creditors, *their* allegiances become subject to the "power of investors ... to switch quickly from one investment to another if 'confidence' is lost" (ibid., p. 88) and in this way even states are obliged to adjust their behaviour accordingly.

The effects on populations are far from uniform. If investors' rights are to be protected, then myriad hybrids of obligation and obedience operate to ensure their protection in ways that an account of the correlation between legal rights and obligations fails to grasp. For example, the obligation to protect creditors' rights puts thousands of individual and social needs and vulnerabilities to the discipline of "affordability" conditions, whereas purely financial debts are prioritised and serviced as such. The case of Greece in the wake of the financial crash is exemplary in seeing how a national government's creditors took priority over the government's social obligations (Christodoulidis 2017). Even where the foreseeable effects of this prioritisation included widespread immiseration, social dislocation, sales of public assets, and the diminution of life chances through the imposition of pension reductions and rates of 50% youth unemployment, they ranked below the protection of creditors' rights. This situation is not unique to Greece. Unsurprisingly, given their design and purpose, in whatever way the pack of debt obligations is shuffled, indebtedness always seems to turn up aces for the creditors wherever they are. The true sleight of hand (as British Prime Minister David Cameron saw when simultaneously giving lots of government money to the institutions which caused the problem while imposing austerity obligations on the population at large) is to make the public believe that "We're all in this together".

If the inequality-producing effects of indebtedness are clear at the macro level, they are also exemplified in consumption practices which provide perhaps the key contemporary route into personal indebtedness in advanced economies. Here again the combination of creditors' rights and the insertion of citizens into economic practices of obligation and obedience are to be found. There are multiple instances of this, among the most commonplace being the growth in personal credit card debt, pay-day loans, and student debts. These debt-inducing consumption practices are at the same time business opportunities, and they are not limited to luxuries but include meeting such basic human needs as housing and education. The overall effect is create a direct if uneven susceptibility of people to market forces over which they, as individuals, have no autonomous control. The fact that such dependencies are created in the name of market freedoms given juridical form is an irony that materialises for many as simply enforced vulnerability and an inevitable decline in autonomy. And while these clearly have constraining effects on individual economic well-being and opportunity, they also have knock-on effects with respect to political action. As Harvey notes, "'[D]ebt-encumbered homeowners don't go on strike'. Likewise, debt-encumbered students don't cause trouble" (Harvey 2018, p. 435). Thus what was true of states is equally true of individuals: indebtedness succeeds in limiting political possibilities. Or to be more precise, it limits *some* political possibilities to the benefit of other, inegalitarian, political positions.

Let us draw the insights from these sections together. With respect to the indebted populace, we can observe an augmentation and intensification of ties of obligation and obedience across areas of labour, consumption, and domestic life that cannot be properly accounted for in the popular imagery of the "age of rights". For what appears as the primacy of freedom is still in fact secondary. As part of the substitution in "obediential obligations" the combination of the economic "law of value" with the legal structuring of property and debt replaces the "primordial debt" of religion with a socio-economic ecology of obligations every bit as constraining. But the central quality of these obligations remains the same as before: they cannot be bargained about by the parties themselves. Why not? Because despite their appearance at one level as the result of "freedom and engagement" what appears as choice is so in appearance only. As an indebted consumer, or as an employee, tenant, or mortgage holder, one is not in a position to bargain about the ground rules. Indeed, as we have just seen, this is increasingly true even with respect to states. Such widespread diminution of personal and political autonomy was given candid expression by Alan Greenspan, the former chairman of the United States Federal Reserve: "[T]hanks to globalization, policy decisions in the US have largely been replaced by global market forces. National security aside, it hardly makes any difference who will be the next president. The world is governed by market forces" (quoted in Streeck, p. 85). If even democratically elected states have such limitations, what chance do individual consumers or tenants or debtors have? One cannot consume one's way to liberty or autonomy in the face of such circumstances precisely since "market forces" are forces not just metaphorically; as Greenspan emphasises, they *govern*. This is why, in Stair's terms, citizens' freedom and engagement still rely upon pre-given non-negotiable obediential norms; the difference is that they are given not now by God, but by the laws of the market. If in one period citizens could not step out of the realm of religious obligation, now it seems impossible to step out of those of the marketplace. The situation *could* be different, as has historically become the case with religion. But as things stand, the current combination of legal and economic ties in the ecology of obligations secures these "obediential obligations" with an omnipresent force.

In the eighteenth century, "dependency" on the will of others was taken as a reason for excluding people – mainly the poor and women – from participating in politics by getting a vote. Their lack of financial independence was understood to make them liable to undue influence from those on whom they were dependent. As we saw with Kant in Chapter 3, this meant they ought to be considered "merely passive" citizens. And yet it is ironic that now, with financial dependency writ large in our debt culture – constraining governments and private citizens alike – that such dependency is rarely treated as a problematic issue with respect to the meaning of *citizenship*. The point is not that the eighteenth-century property qualification on voting was correct. On the contrary, the problem is rather that while citizens do have equal political rights, the reality of debt dependency is largely *not* thematised as a political issue despite its vastly inegalitarian effects being perfectly clear. The operation of debt may involve trading "incorporeal things", but at some point the obligation always materialises for someone in an "intensely personal" way. And for most people in modern society the reality is that the end of the *vinculum iuris* they have is not in their hands. It is round their necks; and it follows them around unrelentingly, it curtails their freedom, it leads them where the creditor wills. As Birks advised: dwell on that image.

6 Obligations, needs, solidarities

Old and new trajectories

We turn now to the role obligations play in contributing to the well-being of individuals and the communities in which they flourish. For as we have noted in a few places earlier in the book obligations also provide a means by which we organise our lives in ways that foster reciprocity, commitment, and trust. In our personal and social lives, as well as through collective practices and institutions, obligations provide direct or mediated ways of sustaining people's potential for communal well-being. Obligations thus have this distinctive, dual quality: they are the expression and means of constraint and limitation which can, as we saw in the previous chapter, sustain modes of undesired control, discipline, and subjection. But they are also the stuff of loyalty, solidarity, and love. In this respect too they have a historical and social continuity that rights lack. If obligations have a more enduring presence and expansive range than rights, it is because rights attach to practices and communal modes of being that are already saturated with obligations.

In the first section of this chapter we will consider how the operation of legal rights in protecting individual well-being is itself highly reliant on the fulfilment of multiple kinds of obligations. Taking rights seriously, in other words, means taking obligations even more seriously. But we will see that there is a further sense of obligation which has additional dimensions in terms of their purpose and justification. This becomes especially vivid with respect to certain kinds of rights, those commonly identified as social and economic rights. In so far as these rights are understood to mark some of the most fundamental values in a community – education, health, welfare, and so on – the obligations they impose are based on foundational commitments that cannot be explained solely by reference to correlative relations found in law. Since a lack of commitment to this sense of obligation can have predictably damaging social consequences, we need to understand the practical limitations to what justiciable rights and obligations can do in modern capitalist societies with respect to individual and collective well-being. To see beyond such limitations, we need to examine how collective values rely instead on prioritising needs, common goods, and solidarities. To assess the work obligations do with respect to these we will focus on some of the social and institutional conditions that foster and maintain dignity among equals, conditions that prioritise a sense of communal obligation in ways that allow commitments to be inaugurated and to flourish to the common benefit of all.

So juxtaposed to the idea that legal rights and obligations are correlative, an alternative account explores the idea that the primary correlative of obligations is not rights but needs. As the French philosopher Simone Weil argued, "Obligation is concerned with the needs in this world of the souls and bodies of human beings, whoever they may be. For each need there is a corresponding obligation; for each obligation a corresponding need" (Weil 2005, pp. 224–225). Paying attention to this deeper work of obligations points us towards assessing the underpinning values of collective and institutional arrangements, and it also opens up resources for addressing new and pressing contemporary concerns. To develop this insight, this chapter analyses the ways in which needs and obligations together find an articulation in the language of solidarity. Acknowledging the limitations of legal rights and obligations in practice and in theory is not, as was noted in the Introduction, to devalue the benefits the protection of these may offer. But as Weil also argued, rights are best thought of as concepts of the middle range – mediocre, she calls them – for they cannot reach any depth of moral connection. Rather, the notion of a right is linked with "exchange, of measured quantity. It has a commercial flavour, essentially evocative of legal claims and arguments. Rights are always asserted in a tone of contention" (Weil 2005, p. 81). That is part of their effectiveness, of course, and the interests they protect are secured by the force required to ensure correlative obligations are appropriately acted upon. But it is the role and capacity of obligations in making more profound connections that is explored here.

One preliminary aspect often overlooked in reflecting on this is that in creating and sustaining communities which seek to recognise the equal dignity of all members, obligations are owed not just to other people but to the standards and values internal to practices and institutions that give them, and the individual and communal goods they nurture, the opportunity to flourish. Obligations, in other words, bind not just in personal and social relations but through and to institutions; to mentalities and modes of conduct; to ways of approaching problems and collaboratively working out and passing on a critical sense of what is right and wrong, appropriate and inappropriate. The standards and values of academic or scientific enquiry for example are learned and transmitted through internalising the obligations of scholarship and collegiality in institutional settings. This sense of obligation, one that comes from an awareness that we are collective custodians of traditions of enquiry that have their own standards of excellence and critique, is thus necessary in continuing such traditions into the future. In this respect they are like other, more personal and informal practices in which obligations provide an important way of transmitting standards and expectations. This is perhaps why in all these settings it is not uncommon to find, albeit in a way different from its economic uses, the language of indebtedness: just as we are indebted to others – family, teachers, friends – for our emotional and intellectual development and well-being, so we too owe obligations to pass on the possibility of well-being to others, including those with whom we have no direct connection, through practices that sustain recognition, common values, and solidarity. It is through these forms and commitments that communities sustain a sense of equal worth and possibility, sometimes in the face of organised and humiliating attacks on communal values and commitments. Rights claims may have some strategic contingent function in this regard, but they appear to have less of a foundational role in understanding the nature of such collective practices as a whole. To think of many of the obligations we learn about or incur in everyday settings – through institutions or practices such as education and enquiry, or through relationships with family, friends, neighbours, and so on – in terms of rights does not seem to do full justice to their character. The vibrancy, and the vulnerability, of those social relations and practices thus benefits from a renewed focus on the work of obligations.

The same is also true when we contemplate a range of further questions that bear on relations between people and the ecological conditions that sustain all human communities. In the last part of this chapter we consider a final example, one that returns us to the language of ecology and obligation but this time in a direct, non-metaphorical way. For arguably the work of obligations is nowhere more important than in thinking about how to respond urgently to the humanly caused environmental degradation that is already a major threat to animal and plant life globally. Here the language and effectiveness of rights may be considered not only inadequate but part of the problem. In considering questions such as these: "Do we have obligations to future generations?"; "Do we have obligations to stop harming the environment?"; "Do we have obligations to make communities near and far ecologically better places for those who live in them?", we may ask whether such obligations would exist only because they – these persons or things – have correlative rights. If the answer to the latter question is *No*, then it would seem to suggest that obligations across time in these settings rely on some other, non-rights-based justifications. If the answer is *Yes* – there are only such obligations if there are correlative rights – we might want to examine the reasoning, prospects, and perhaps even the mind-set, that this relied on. For arguably it would be like answering the question "Do I have obligations towards my children?", with another, one that demanded to know first: "What rights to do they have?" This would be a peculiar form of reasoning. The chapter thus closes by considering whether, with respect to the environment, certain non-negotiable obligations need to be identified and instantiated as "necessary obligations" of the kind identified in Chapter 1.

Taking obligations seriously

It is a commonplace in legal analysis to observe that there is a necessary correlation between legal rights and obligations: that each right has a corresponding obligation and therefore that there is a constant and direct relation between particular rights and obligations. (The full complexities of this are set out in Hohfeld 1964.) It was pointed out in Chapter 1 that there is a historical contingency to this understanding that is often overlooked, and, as we have just seen, it does not necessarily provide an accurate portrayal of the role of obligations generally across social practices. But even with respect to legal rights and obligations we find another kind of reason why the correlative account might be problematic. Jeremy Waldron argues that when we consider rights, even basic "negative" or "liberty" rights, we encounter what he calls "waves of duties", a phenomenon that puts to question a straightforward notion of correlativity. He gives the example of the right not to be tortured. On one reading this would correlate simply to a single duty on another person not to inflict torture, and that their inaction in this regard would be sufficient to respect that right. Yet one person's right correlates to the duty on countless others not to torture and in that sense there are far more duties than rights. But that obvious point is not what Waldron is getting at. Rather, he argues, we cannot fully understand the operation of this right in practice unless we see that the same right generates not just one duty of this sort, but of multiple *kinds* of duties (hence the "waves" image). So the duty not to torture is, he writes,

> backed up by other duties: a duty to instruct people about the wrongness of torture; a duty to be vigilant about the danger of, and temptation to, torture; a duty to ameliorate situations in which torture might be thought likely to occur; and so on.
>
> (Waldron 1989, p. 510)

And then, should torture in fact be alleged, there are duties to investigate, duties to hold perpetrators to account, to provide remedies, to change practices to avoid likely repetition, and so on. Flowing from the right not to be tortured, in other words, there are successive "waves of duty" that signal not just that there are many more (and different) duties arising than rights but also that this *has* to be the case if rights themselves are to be taken seriously. Moreover, in order that all these duties are generally met, the actions required signal that resources are necessary to ensure their performance. In this sense rights, even negative liberty rights – the right to be left free from being tortured, say, or the right to free speech or association – have real costs associated with them.

This is the case with social and economic rights too. The right to education, for example, can only be equally secured throughout a large society by the positive action of many others. Typically, this will involve assigning obligations to a range of actors, individuals, and institutions. So, an individual's right to education will require for its protection obligations on government officials and local authorities to assign adequate resources to fund schools at various levels. Schools and teachers will in turn have a wide range of obligations imposed on them by state and professional bodies. There will then be further obligations to establish everything from assessment schemes to student safety procedures, and so on. Fulfilling the right to education therefore requires these multiple levels and instances of obligation, without which the right would in practice likely be meaningless. There is, moreover, a temporal – or dynamic – aspect that is important here. Hence the same right can result not only in numerous and different obligations on multiple actors, but these obligations and actors may change over time with respect to the same right (Raz 1986, p. 171). The idea that rights and obligations are established in a "once and for all", categorical manner neglects the basic experience and understanding of how communities learn over time in and through practices and that upholding rights requires changing and developing expectations and obligations of actors and institutions. A static model of rights tends to miss much of this dynamic activity. This is especially clear in the context of socio-economic rights where the experience of practising in a needs-based institutional process provides conditions whereby obligations change through learning over time. To fail to account for this experience – the experience of what Atria calls, drawing on Charles Taylor, "slow pedagogy" – is to downplay the value of learning, in common, in shared practices over time. It is also, therefore, to risk negating the developing benefits this brings, including the benefits to rights protection itself (Atria 2015).

So even if a list of rights as entitlements stays relatively stable, "waves of obligations" continue to be required to do justice to them in a way that is not captured by a straightforward and abstract "correlative" account of the relation between legal rights and obligations. The individual and communal goods that rights may help to protect are reliant on the regular, dynamic, and complex work of obligations. Indeed, to the extent that there has been an augmentation in rights-talk and rights-practice, this has unleashed an even greater proliferation of obligations of many kinds and at many levels. This cannot therefore be merely a matter of describing the same correlative relation in a different way. A sociologically grounded sensibility to the conceptual and institutional conditions in which rights are protected indicates that it is the fulfilment of obligations that more adequately explains the workings of a wide range of contemporary social and institutional practices.

That said, the matter of which perspective to prioritise with respect to rights and obligations may have additional and significant implications. Onora O'Neill makes several important observations in this regard. First, she argues that while the contemporary rhetoric of rights has, as she puts it, a certain charm, part of that charm derives from the fact that such rhetoric can be "deeply evasive". The reason for this is that when we think about justice, say, in terms of the primacy of rights "we are more or less bound to find not only that we do not or cannot live up to [the rhetoric], but that we cannot work out what we are trying to live up to" (O'Neill 2000, p. 97). In an article discussing "women's rights", but also with respect to rights generally, O'Neill argues that starting with rights offers a "lopsided way of thinking about ethics, and even about justice" since it "systematically obscures what we would most need to think about and do if we were to take rights seriously" (ibid., pp. 98–99). What is missing, in essence, is a coherent account of obligations.

O'Neill develops the point further in the context of socio-economic rights arguing that a focus on rights underplays the vital but difficult work required to actually make rights effective. To do this again requires paying attention to the operationalisation of many more obligations than rights as well as specifying "which obligation bearers are going to have to do what, for whom and at what cost" (p. 103). This, she says, "is a much less charming topic" (p. 100). Thus both negative rights, such as the right not to be tortured, and socio-economic rights, such as the right to education or healthcare – what O'Neill calls rights to goods and services – entail not only the identification of obligated actors but also obligations of distributive justice in the resource allocation necessary to provide the requisite institutional support. As O'Neill notes:

> Rights to goods and services are easy to proclaim, but until there are effective institutions their proclamation may seem bitter mockery to those who most need them ... By contrast, when we discuss obligations, of whatever sort, we immediately have to consider *whose* obligations we have in mind and so will define *against whom* rights-holders may lodge their claims.
>
> (p. 105, emphasis in original)

Otherwise, a claimant "will not know where to press her claim, and it will be systematically obscure whether there is any perpetrator, or who has neglected or violated her rights" (ibid.).

O'Neill's point is not to endorse a straightforward critique of rights, and particularly one aimed at "socio-economic" rights. In fact, as we have noted, her point is that unless and until we take obligations seriously, we cannot in fact take such rights seriously. This is especially significant with respect to rights to goods and services which are commonly more vulnerable to neglect, particularly in circumstances where poverty and inequalities are widespread. To understand why, it is worth pausing to note the language O'Neill used in the line just quoted: "whether there is any perpetrator". There appears at first to be something awkward, something out of place about the language of "perpetrator" when it comes to not delivering on rights to goods and services; the use of this language seems more appropriate to violators of individual liberties or rights to bodily integrity, say. But this is precisely the point: starting from the perspective of the right, one has difficulty taking the institutional and socio-economic conditions that fail to secure goods and services as conditions in which *perpetrators* violate the entitlements rights are supposed to protect. One major reason for this is that delivering on these goods and services requires the co-ordinated activities of numerous people fulfilling obligation-based roles within complex institutional practices. This makes it difficult to attribute even the fulfilment of entitlements to a specific person. And so when the entitlements are not adequately protected – where housing or maternity or children's rights are not met, for example – the same structures of delivery make it difficult to establish the existence of a "perpetrator" who infringes the right. No one individual intentionally violated the rights holder's entitlement, and, cumulatively, there is no overall responsibility for the failure to meet those needs that remain unmet (see Veitch 2007, ch 2).

If the language of perpetrators seems inadequate, this is perhaps because it fails to address a further underlying problem. This is one we saw identified by South African judge Edwin Cameron in Chapter 3. Even where a constitutional democracy contains a Bill of Rights of the most progressive kind, this can, and does, he said, co-exist with "rampant inequality, dispossession, injustice and exclusion". Such conditions are not unique to South Africa, but operate in most developed economies where social and economic rights to goods and services are given legal and even constitutional protection yet these continue to co-exist with the unnecessary suffering that poverty, discrimination, and inequality exacerbate. It is not a lack of stated rights, in other words, that is the problem. Rather, as David Garland points out, such rights "have been established in the legal systems of many capitalist nations for more than half a century, without noticeably disruptive or revolutionary effects" (quoted in Christodoulidis 2017, p. 132). It is as if, to return to the ancient image, the *vinculum iuris* that would bind parties can find no attachment; the rights holder cannot secure the other end of the rope to any other legal person. So where the rhetoric of rights "takes the perspective of the claimant rather than of the contributor, of the consumer rather than of the producer, of the passive rather than of the active citizen" (O'Neill 2000, p. 101) the stark reality is that in unequal societies, claimants' rights are met, if they are at all, in systematically uneven ways that mirror and predictably reproduce patterns of social inequality. It is precisely this state of affairs that seems to make "bitter mockery" of the promise these rights hold out. To shift perspective then from rights to obligations means not only making commitments to harnessing multiple (waves of) obligations. It also involves a re-assessment of what the second of each of these pairs – contributor, producer, active citizen – means with respect to the primacy of *collective* obligations. It requires seeing that such obligations function on a different basis from those that would further rights protection. On this alternative view, taking obligations seriously in institutional practices is not merely a means of taking rights seriously, but of taking other *obligations* seriously. And these obligations are not those that correlate to rights, but mark out something more fundamental.

Needs and obligations

One way to address this is to consider more closely the shift in understanding that follows from seeing obligations as correlative to needs rather than rights. This was the suggestion we drew from Simone Weil at the start of this chapter. Let us now consider in more detail some aspects to this position.

The starting point is the observation that human vulnerabilities and dependencies are such that everyone has needs that must be met if we are to live and have the chance of living in a way we think worthwhile. Complex societies like our own address needs directly and in mediated ways, through a multifaceted division of labour. Meeting material needs, for instance, the provision of food for our daily meals, relies on countless people and technologies, most of them unknown and invisible to us but without which we would fare very poorly very quickly. Other needs combine material and intellectual aspects associated with a sense of human development over time. As young people growing up, for example, we are entirely reliant on adults – primarily parents, wider family, and friends, but also teachers, nurses, doctors, and so on – who feed and shelter and care for us but who also, if we are fortunate, respond to and encourage our sense of wonder, and thereby educate us and allow us to be educated. A major part of this involves addressing the need we have to relate well to other people, and thus we rely on others to inspire insight and reflection especially when there is hurt or uncertainty; to respond to and maintain a sense of hope and possibilities; to encourage a sense of the dignity of others and ourselves, and a sensitivity to cruelty and to the harm of humiliation; to help us find a voice to speak with and express sympathy with others.

In each of these senses, we are all equal in needs. And these needs are both individual *and* collective. In the first place, because we cannot do these things on our own; we need others to meet our own and others' needs whether these are material or emotional or intellectual. Importantly, however, needs are not something we can overcome when a certain degree of maturity or relative independence is reached; needs have an enduring presence. For it is an ineliminable part of the human condition to be vulnerable and dependent throughout our lives. This is something from which no person is exempted since everyone, albeit in different ways and at different times in their lives, will have needs as a consequence of illness, injury, disability, or the infirmities of old age. With respect to all these, there is little possibility but to rely on others for help in meeting our needs. As such, it is, argues Alasdair MacIntyre, a community's response to such vulnerabilities that provides "an important index of the flourishing of the whole community. It is in so far as it is *need* that provides reasons for action for the members of some particular community that that community flourishes" (MacIntyre 1999, p. 109, emphasis in original).

One important feature of this situation is that communities will necessarily rely on what he calls "relationships of uncalculated giving and receiving". These are "uncalculated" in the sense that "we can rely on no strict proportionality of giving and receiving" (ibid., pp. 117, 126). Needs change over time and so does the capacity of our self and others to respond to them. So even if there is in one sense a fundamental equality to the inescapability of need, in another sense what people are called on to do for others changes with circumstance and ability. People give or receive more at some points than others, and also respond to others in ways that are not necessarily, and in fact not usually, symmetrical. These relationships are therefore not such as to be reducible to some proportionality of exchange, of "trading advantage for advantage" (ibid., p. 108). Such "calculation" would systematically misunderstand and thus be incapable of doing justice to the shifting nature of needs and capacities. Yet without these relationships, without meeting the responsibilities that inhere in such relationships as they change over time and circumstance, communities would likely not endure, never mind flourish.

The individual and collective nature of needs requires that they are met in a wide variety of ways. Some are more local or intimate. Others involve institutional arrangements that instantiate more or less hierarchical responsibilities of role that are not, or not usually, dependent on personal connections. Thus schools and hospitals and other organisations that form part of a complex welfare state commonly deploy impersonal and bureaucratic means to meet individual and community needs. In making this connection, however, such institutional forms – those "hard-won machineries of compassion" as William McIllvanney (1991, p. 134) expertly describes them – deliver a community's response to the needs of others. But what role do obligations play in these needs-based practices? And how might obligations relate to needs in ways that a discourse of rights does not adequately address?

In *The Needs of Strangers* Michael Ignatieff observes that "[q]uestions about human needs *are* questions about human obligations" (Ignatieff 1984, p. 27, emphasis added). Like Weil, he claims that it is needs and their corresponding obligations that have a priority in thinking about communal relations among equals. And while for him rights have some role to play, that role is essentially one of being an institutional trigger for someone or some body to act. They do not provide the foundational, justificatory basis of the obligation to respond. Discussing the role of the welfare state in modern society he thus traces the connections in these terms: "It is this solidarity among strangers, this transformation through the division of labour of needs into rights and rights into care that gives us whatever fragile basis we have for saying that we live in a moral community" (Ignatieff 1984, p. 10). On this view needs, and corresponding obligations, form the primary social relation and rights are best understood as intermediate mechanisms that work to deliver in a more or less satisfactory way on the priority of needs and the obligation to respond to them.

But, as Ignatieff further argues, rights have a limited capability in a deeper sense. Echoing the observations made earlier, he notes: "Rights language offers a rich vernacular for the claims an individual may make on or against the collectivity, but it is relatively impoverished as a means of expressing individuals' needs *for* the collectivity" (ibid., p. 13, emphasis in original). Although rights language speaks the values of universal humanity and equality, not all needs, and perhaps the most fundamental of them – for "love, respect, honour, dignity, solidarity with others" (ibid., p. 15) – can be addressed through the language of rights. On the one hand, it is perfectly possible, as we have seen, for societies to recognise rights, and to treat them as justiciable, but to be more or less incapable of caring for their members' needs. Part of the reason for this is that the language of rights, as Ignatieff puts it,

> can only express the human ideal of fraternity as mutual respect for *rights*, and it can only defend the claim to be treated with dignity in terms of our common identity as rights-bearing creatures, and there is more to respect in a person than his rights.
> (ibid., emphasis added)

On the other hand, given that "any decent society requires a public discourse about the needs of the human person" (ibid., p. 13) it is this "public" dimension that allows us to note a more fundamental incapacity to rights. For what Ignatieff identified as individuals' needs *for* the collectivity means that understanding the fundamental relations necessary for human flourishing within a community requires responding to their irreducibly collective dimension in a way that rights, even socio-economic rights, do not capture. This is not a critique of rights as such, but rather a mark of their limitation. The reason for this is that the public discourse refers not only or primarily to needs' affective, emotional, or even material presence. Rather, it indicates that the obligation to respond to needs has to be understood primarily as a collective obligation and, precisely *as* collective, it is at root a matter of politics and not of legal determination. As Ignatieff puts it, "The deepest motivational springs of political involvement are to be located in this human capacity to feel needs for others" (ibid., p. 17). And in this scenario rights would come – if they come at all: we recall they are an essentially modern, Western invention – at the *end* of a process of reasoning, not the start.

There is then a politics to the identification of and responses to what obligations a community has not just in terms of material needs but those of the cultural and communal needs required for individual and collective flourishing. We will see in more detail shortly why, and how, this insight suggests that needs and obligations are connected to solidarity. But it is worth pausing at this point to note a challenge to this way of understanding the priority of needs. Rejecting a needs-based approach Jeremy Waldron makes a number of claims. In a way consistent with the analysis just made, needs, he acknowledges, generate "active responsibilities: duties to give, duties to assist, duties to rescue" (Waldron 2000, p. 125). But he differs in assessing what that relationship means, and what it entails with respect to obligations. On the one hand, for Waldron, "the modern language of needs ... has dimensions of confessional and therapeutic narcissism ... exploited by its users for the intensification of their demands". Those who are "needy", he argues, are often self-centred, manipulative of others to fulfil their desires, or are lacking in self-sufficiency. "Needs-talk", he concludes, "is the language of supplicants". By contrast, "those who are looking after their own necessities find other ways of expressing themselves" (ibid., p. 123). On the other hand, rather than "the duty to *mind one's own business* ... the duties generated by needs require me to *go out of my way* to help you". These duties – "to *attend to*, or *be sensitive to* another's position" (ibid., pp. 125–126, emphases in original) – can be contrasted with those correlating to "traditional" rights where "everyone is simply to be left alone [and] no special sensitivity is called for" (ibid., p. 126). On this view, the rights-bearer is "self-aware and vigorously conscious of what she is entitled to demand from others" (ibid., p. 130).

In one sense Waldron is correct – rights do not do this work of attention directly, which is precisely their limit. But that is equally why the needs-obligation nexus is a foundational matter for both individual and collective activity in sustaining communities where the worth of all is valued. Where Waldron's position is suspect is that by over-emphasising his critique of this nexus, it portrays the mainsprings and the experience of human interaction in an almost unrecognisable way. It lacks an appreciation of the equal but variable nature of vulnerabilities and dependencies as a constant feature of communal life. It seems to give expression to an illusion that MacIntyre identifies in these terms: "We recognize here an illusion of self-sufficiency ... that is all too characteristic of the rich and powerful", an illusion which, he adds, "plays its part in excluding them from certain types of communal relationship" (MacIntyre 1999, p. 127). What it fails to see is that "needs-talk" *is* the language of equals, and in that sense we are all "supplicants", including for positive, life-enhancing opportunities – for care, love, learning, aesthetic experience, and so on. Of course, our vulnerabilities and dependencies do not describe all that we are or can be. The point of treating the needs-based account as foundational is that it is only by recognising people's individual and collective needs as a priority that allows them the potential to become less vulnerable and less dependent. Without prioritising needs and the obligations required to respond to them, our experience would be highly circumscribed and our visions narrow, mean, and consistently unequal. For this – the matter of equality and inequality – is also why the nexus of needs and obligations is a political concern, since it involves power and its distribution as a collective matter, and is thus best attended to by collective deliberation and responsibility. It is for this reason too that the language of solidarity is relevant.

Obligations and solidarities

The term solidarity has its roots in Roman Law:

> *obligatio in solidum* defines the status of joint liability for a financial debt ... To be in solidarity means that a man is good for his debts and stands up to his obligations to others even when he has not benefited from them directly. To be the cosignatory of a loan means that one is liable for the reversals of fortune of another; that one's own economic well-being is no longer completely in one's own hands.
>
> (Pensky 2008, p. 6)

What is significant about this lineage is that while solidarity is sometimes considered to be overly particularistic and affective, there is an important sense in which

> [n]either genes nor love, but *liability* is the bonding force. We are bound together with those with whom, like it or not, our own fates and our own well-being are interwoven. That, and not a sum of money to be repaid, is the sense of the acknowledgment of debt.
> (ibid., emphasis added)

Solidarity has a range of contemporary meanings. But it is primarily that notion of "joint liability" that captures its intimate relation with obligation. Since "liability" shares its linguistic heritage with *ligare* (and the French *lier*) (Birks 2014, p. 3) the connection it has with that which binds is in one sense clear enough. The primary relation is thus that of a bond: bound to sharing risks, responsibilities, and so on. In a way that recognises that "our own fates and our own well-being are interwoven" our interest here is not so much with individual creditors and debtors, but an extended sense of how a collective is bound together; the social bond in which the collective becomes greater than the sum of its individual parts through the existence of joint liabilities. Importantly, this does not mean that solidarities involve only "the binding together of pre-existing communities", where membership relies on the similarities of participants (Featherstone 2012, p. 7). Rather, solidaristic communities may be "expansive and not bounded within particular groups" since they are "actively produced and shaped" through dynamic processes of deliberation and even contestation (ibid., pp. 22–23). Building solidarities is thus a process of constructing forms of community bound together through collective engagement and activity that produces a shared sense of responsibility, a recognition of the common dependency that lies at the core of the social bond.

In this sense solidarity resonates with the language of the common good. The common good does not mean that all participants have only identical interests. Their interests may vary among themselves and over time. Just as needs differ and change as people pass through various stages of vulnerability and dependency, likewise participants' contributions to the common good are not all or always the same but change, particularly as they grow in experience and responsibility. Importantly, what participants do all share, whatever the particular content of the common good, is a commitment to something more than themselves – more *in* themselves – than their own individual interests or their satisfaction, or even these individual interests aggregated together. What is done in and for the common good is what needs to be done to sustain that which is *common*. Thus acting for the sake of others is a central obligation in thinking about how to act for the common good. This does not negate individual goods. Rather, the relationship between the common good and individual goods can best be explained in this way: "[W]e become neither self-rather-than-other-regarding nor other-rather-than-self-regarding, neither egoists nor altruists, but those whose passions and inclinations are directed to what is *both our good and the goods of others*" (MacIntyre 1999, p. 160, emphasis added). In any large community there will likely be a plurality of common goods, goods that exist within practices, associations, and institutions. Within these the common good is furthered not only by means of shared goals, but bonds of solidary obligation captured by the idea of joint liability. Indeed, the term "community" contains this "obligatory" dimension within it. The *munis* component of *com-munis* originally referred to the obligations that came with public office, carried out by those citizens in Rome whose honour it was to have been selected as holders of official positions. It thus signified a form of binding association rooted in the obligations of service among citizens in a reciprocal manner. This sense of "[h]e who has *munia* in common", writes Benveniste, "determines a 'community', a group of persons united by this bond of reciprocity" (Benveniste 1973, p. 69). It is the achievement of this unity through reciprocities of mutually bound actions that marked the identity of a group as a community, something expressed well in the variant reading of *communis* as com-*unis*, united, as one (Williams 1988, p. 70).

Drawing together these points, as it may be understood today, solidarity consists in bonds of reciprocity, mutual trust, and respect for dignity among equals that respond to the ineliminable needs, vulnerabilities, and dependencies we have in common. As such, relations of solidarity cannot be built on foundations of exploitation. Solidarity's primary *locus* is the collective, and its *telos* is the common good. It is the contribution of obligations to developing and sustaining collective commitments, joint liabilities, and the social bond over time that provides resources for ties of solidarity to flourish. In this sense they have the characteristic of being what Christodoulidis (following Supiot 2007) calls *dogmatic*. As he puts it: "The *non-negotiability* of the fundamental values of reciprocity, solidarity, and community that underlie what it means to *belong* in a world are installed and enshrined at the level of the dogmatic as the mainsprings of obligation"

(Christodoulidis 2018, p. 6, emphases in original). And these dogmatic or foundational characteristics are, as we have seen, best understood as responses to fundamental needs.

To concretise these observations let us consider three places or levels at which such solidary obligations can be seen in modern societies: the level of the state, of sub-state or civil society, and in ties across borders. Each brings out different features and facets of solidarity within which obligations work to structure community relations.

At the state level a key expression of joint liability can be found in the fiscal system, where the legal obligation to pay taxes instantiates a sense of solidarity as a matter of distributive justice. Typical of welfare states that seek to supply common goods on the basis of need and not the ability to pay – in education and health, for example – resources are pooled so that risks and liabilities are shared. Gallagher summarises this well, noting both the priority of need and the obligations attendant on this:

> Pooling tax receipts to support public expenditure across the country means spending can be determined by need, not by where the tax money comes from ... Poor areas shouldn't have rotten public services simply because they do not have a strong local tax base ... Taxation should be redirected to support pensions, benefits and public services where needed.
>
> (Gallagher 2013, p. 4)

And what determines the level of taxation due by any citizen, at least in a system where progressive taxation exists, is the principle of the ability to pay. The overall effect of this can thus be explained in the following terms: "Fiscal sharing both demands and creates a sense of common obligation. Economic integration connects with social solidarity. Sharing of resources requires and reinforces a sense of belonging and it creates a common social citizenship" (ibid.).

Acting on this sense of common obligation is a major reason why those – typically with much wealth – who avoid fiscal responsibilities by diverting their wealth through complex legal mechanisms such as offshore tax havens are widely condemned for doing so, since they fail their communities in at least two ways. First, they avoid obligations to contribute to the common pool of resources despite their wealth having been generated within that jurisdiction, and, when they are fully capable of contributing their share. And, second, they nonetheless rely on the fiscal contributions of *other* citizens to that common pool to supply many of the infrastructural conditions and personnel necessary for wealth generation in the first place. In seeking to make themselves individually immune from such fiscal liabilities, and hence from the needs these help address, they fail in their communal, solidary obligations. By contrast, the principle of joint liability may be well stated in these terms:

> To understand solidarity as the foundation of the social state, and the founding commitment to mutualize the risks of existence through the provision of social protection, is to appreciate the gesture that understands societal valorization as *irreducibly collective*, where even those less exposed to risks bear a responsibility, given that they partake as beneficiaries of the totality of social production.
> (Christodoulidis 2017, p. 128, emphasis added)

At a second level are the multiple associations and institutions located outside the more formally defined political relations between citizens and the state. Such associations play a major part in integrating people within communities, situating them among a range of collective practices pursuing common goods, and instituting values not reducible to those of either the state or the market. Organised in more or less horizontal and autonomous ways, they may rely on internal hierarchies of roles and responsibilities and involve many and varied types of activity, from collective deliberation and resource allocation to sustaining and even re-framing community concerns. Through these are valorised the kinds of experience, skills, and virtues that are typically not accessible through citizens' direct relations with the state. As well as playing formative and ongoing roles in communities, they may also be called on in part to play defensive roles against dominant state or economic institutions and policies. As Maurice Glasman, drawing on Polanyi, explains, "Societal institutions protect the cultural resources of society from depletion and exhaustion by regulating [social] production and educating the person" (Glasman 1996, p. 6). One of the main functions of such associations is thus to generate and maintain communal activities in ways that institute obligations within solidaristic processes and outcomes. As voluntary obligations, participants may enjoy being subject to them, but they are obligations nonetheless and thus form an important part of a society's ecology of obligations. Glasman also captures their relation to solidarity well: since society is

> characterized by a dependence on others for survival ... this demand[s] a shared responsibility for their fate ... [S]olidarity stresses

the constraints on freedom resulting from dependency and the institutions necessary to prevent the necessity of association from becoming a form domination.

(Glasman 1996, p. 41)

Often the major challenge to such associations is that the cultural resources – the associations and institutions that would protect the fragility and the potential of formative social relationships – have *themselves* been made vulnerable to or been taken over by the very logics – particularly those of the market – they were supposed to protect society from. Whether in artistic, sporting, educational, or cultural associations, or in formerly public or shared spaces, it is not common goods but market competitiveness which has been imposed from outside and practices re-oriented towards that end. Where this occurs shared responsibility becomes increasingly vulnerable to the logic of individualised profit generation and the practices of asymmetrical obedience we addressed in earlier chapters. These financial imperatives are typically generated by market players insinuating themselves across a range of practices, supported in doing so by both party political ideologues and what C Wright Mills described as an "astounding volume of propaganda for commodities" (Mills 1956, p. 356). No area of social activity is taboo from this perspective, whether it is making profit from sickness, the elderly, housing, or the educational and recreational needs of the young. Where this occurs, the solidarity that is possible within these intermediary places is disavowed or transformed and sold back to participants as the mere solidarity of shoppers. And those who seek to profit from them have no other stake – who, given the purpose of their intervention, *can* have no other stake – in the community than their own benefit.

By contrast, obligations within associations that practise solidarity as joint liability express and seek not only common goods, but they are also tempered by standards that recognise and further the equality and dignity of participants as *ends in themselves*. And it is precisely in so far as they are first of all collective activities that solidarity is a register appropriate to their flourishing and through which we may grasp the significance of the obligations that attend them. Solidarity within such collectives or associations might therefore be expressed in the formulation we saw Jefferson stating in the Declaration of Independence. According to this, the justified right and the obligation to act coincide in the practice of a community's self-determination: "It is our right, it is our duty ..." (And in this respect it may be contrasted with the perspective of the market player in their relation to the communities they prey on: "It is our right [to extract surplus value], it is *your* duty [to provide it]".)

Insofar then as such associations are vulnerable to state and especially market logics, we may take note of a final sense of obligation commonly found in them. Communities of solidarity rely on trust, yet participants will recognise that they sometimes need to show a critical distrust towards other modes of operation that would undermine them. In the case of market intervention, for example, there is a solidary obligation to repel commodification for speculative gain; an obligation, in other words, to protect the needs of people rather than the needs of the market where the latter's sole principle of operation seems to be "take as much out as you can while putting as little in as you can and all in the shortest possible time" (McAlpine 2014, p. 117). Where common goods and purposes and the equality of participants in needs-based practices are all vulnerable to the unequal impact of private property differentials that commodification introduces, the obligation to resist such interventions will seek therefore to "decommodif[y] some spheres of common life, so that the unequal distribution of private property does not manifest itself in these spheres". On its own, this communal self-defence will not necessarily transform society as a whole; "[i]nequalities [will] not disappear", but at least they will be "restricted to a limited area of consumption" (Atria and Salgado 2019, p. 377).

This brings us to a third level at which we may consider communities of solidarity. Solidarity can also be seen extending beyond local collectives or national borders. The sense of joint liability usually takes on different aspects here. For example, where the lives of others in different parts of the world are being humiliated by exploitation, injustice, or inequalities, it is possible to write a final variation of Jefferson's right/duty formulation: "It is *your* right, it is *our* duty ..." to bear witness, provide support, raise awareness, agitate, protest, and so on. Common loyalties are often garnered or strengthened in their results by the actions of those who feel obliged to act in solidarity since others' exploitation and suffering are intolerable to them. A sense of obligation to act with and for others is not thereby limited by national borders. When there are harmful or discriminatory practices – of race, gender, or labour exploitation, say – in different geographical locations, then "political solidarity is *not* coterminous with the boundaries of nation states" (Kerruish and Hunt 1992, p. 231, emphasis added). To act as if it was would falsely prioritise these borders and make it more difficult both to appreciate that commonalities do exist across such boundaries and, with respect to harms suffered as a result of these practices, to see that the appropriate locus of response is one that tracks the needs arising from them with obligations of solidarity. Indeed, when it comes to exploitation, there may be much more commonality *across* borders than there is within in them. And so, rather than "political allegiance [being] given first and foremost to the political community of the nation state", the contrary principle is one "which requires solidarity within and across nation states with those with whom some standpoint is shared" (ibid., p. 233). Such solidarity registers a refusal to treat political obligations within a state as always or necessarily having priority over other obligations, and instead understands that bonds of obligation transcend jurisdictional boundaries.

From these observations we can see a variation of a formulation noted earlier: that "waves of obligations" may be understood as operating not only as a means of taking rights seriously; they also operate as a means of taking other obligations seriously. As Candice Delmas has argued, for example, with respect to the obligation to respect people's dignity, a number of further, "second order" obligations flow from this. As she writes:

> [D]ignity supports a general obligation to *resist* one's and others' violations of dignity. People who are not treated as equal and valuable members of their community – who are socially or politically subservient – have an ethical obligation (owed to themselves) to resist their own mistreatment; and members of a polity that violates some of its members' dignity have a moral obligation (owed to others) to resist such mistreatment.
> (Delmas 2016, pp. 32–33, emphasis in original)

These obligations to resist, argues Delmas, can take many forms, from protests and strikes to acts of civil disobedience and violent struggle, depending on "the kind and magnitude of the indignity threatened, and on the agent's abilities, opportunities, and particular position relative to the indignity" (ibid., p. 33). And that these obligations constitute part of the discourse and practice of solidarity is clear. As she concludes, "Solidarity in resistance is a crucial way of expressing proper concern for everyone, and should be viewed as a moral obligation of both subordinated and privileged members of society" (ibid., p. 38).

Seen then through the lens of solidarity, the relations within and among communities near and distant – of politics as collective action geared towards common goods, and shared liabilities internal to and across borders – allows us to understand the work of obligations in a different light. The demands of and for solidarity deploy alternative ways of thinking about the need for and the potential of collective action, particularly where threats to dignity and equality arise. Oftentimes, the mainsprings of such action can be found already existing within the reservoirs of solidarity familiar from localised experiences, in what Rogan calls the "unheralded promise in everyday settings" (Rogan 2017, p. 7). In that sense, there are older and ongoing trajectories of obligation embedded in the "relationships of uncalculated giving and receiving" MacIntyre identified as so important. But in so far as these come up against new challenges, and as new opportunities also open up, then there are new trajectories to be thought of too. It is this possibility we turn to in the final section.

Ecology *and* obligations

The greatest dangers facing societies globally are now all human-made: extreme inequalities which continue to produce deathly results on an industrial scale; the maintenance and threatened use of nuclear weapons by a handful of states (including the five permanent members of the UN Security Council which is responsible for world peace and security), the budget for which is staggering for technologies whose only use is to murder millions of innocents; and the environmental destruction that eats up ever faster the future time of human and much plant and animal life. In each scenario it does not seem that discourses of rights are helping to address the dangers. Severe and growing inequalities are largely the result of a system of global production, consumption, and distribution which is protected by a complex regime of property rights that is working, not failing. The legality of threatening mass extinction through the firing of nuclear weapons at "enemy" populations is guaranteed in international law by the sovereign state's right to self-defence (Veitch 2007, pp. 117ff). And the human inhabitants of an emphysemic earth are slowly waking up to their burning-spree hangover of planetary proportions – to the scars and cuts, to things irretrievably lost: species, habitats – and seem simply incapable, under current dynamics, of setting up an international rights regime that would have any remedial impact on the situation whatsoever. Perhaps the greatest challenge here lies in facing up to the fact that when it comes to environmental destruction, political and legal common sense as they currently exist are straightforwardly disastrous. Jonathan Schell expresses this vividly, addressing the role of sovereign rights in the international state system, and it applies more generally: "We are told that 'realism' compels us to preserve the system of sovereignty. But that political realism is not biological realism; it is biological nihilism – and for that reason it is, of course, political nihilism, too" (Schell 1982, p. 218).

When "morality bottoms out at the top" (Amis 1988, p. 6), if there is to be a longer term then an alternative vision is plainly necessary. What that might involve is still undefined, and it may never take shape if the present conditions persist much longer. But the force of obligations – of binding people to each other and to things: the earth, nature, the future – is one form that some part of it might take. Along with a certain humility and solidarity in the recognition of our own and our neighbours' ecological vulnerabilities and dependencies, near and far, as well as a fierce defence of each person's dignity, the binding of people and institutions to standards required to address these dangers seems vital. This can and should be done without waiting for a full-blown theory of rights to be invented, justified, and set in place, not least because whatever this might look like would likely end up being more of the same where the economic and political conditions remain largely undisturbed. In particular, capitalism's relentless blind momentum for growth makes it constitutively unable to understand any obligation to slow down to care for the environment. This is a double blindness in that not only can it not see this fundamental problematic, but it cannot see that it cannot see it. For if it could not care less, nor could it care more. The exploitation and commodification of all and any "resources" – human, plant, animal, organic and inorganic – for the sake of profit means this mode of production is unable to redress environmental degradation on the latter's terms. Indeed, if profit can be made out of anything, environmental damage offers just another business opportunity. No amount of attaching obligations to capitalist relations of exchange or property rights (such as in land or energy) will be able to redress the harms or compensate for them. One cannot imagine an equivalent to the Ogden Tables – used in England and Wales to calculate the amount of monetary compensation due in personal injuries claims – that incorporated damages and variables such as species lost, global temperature rises, continental drought, rise in sea levels, etc. Or, rather, *only* a capitalist legal system could imagine and come up with such tables, which gives some indication of the problem.

A lot more has been and needs to be said about this, not least with respect to the still neglected importance of non-Western modes of seeing human relations as part of the natural world. But in closing let us consider one way of thinking that invokes obligation as central to building solidary responses to environmental destruction. According to this view, a re-prioritisation of obligations is a necessary corrective in overcoming the limitations of modern legal and political thinking. For the latter treats the natural world as a mere "backdrop" against which human institutions operate; as something external to human organisations, to be acted *on*, and – emblematically in classical social contract thinking – as a condition, the "state of nature", to be left behind in order to establish "civilization". But now, where human action has impacted upon the environment to such an extent that it has palpably changed climatic conditions, "the backdrop is beginning to move, the scenery and props have come to life" (Matthews 2019, p. 667). Rising global temperatures and sea levels, increasing extreme weather conditions, acidification, ozone layer depletion, and the other conditions associated with the Anthropocene are results, some potentially irreversible now, of human activities. In addressing these conditions some have been inspired by the idea of the "rights of nature", resulting in aspirational claims including the Universal Declaration of the Rights of Mother Earth and the Universal Declaration on River Rights. But the weakness of such approaches is, according to Matthews, that for all their apparent innovative impetus it "is really a continuation of one of the central tenets of the modern project that sees the institutionalization of a justiciable right as a fundamental goal of political action" (ibid., p. 686). By contrast, Matthews argues, awareness of the Anthropocene signals the need for a radical re-thinking of or even departure from such modern categories and modes of organisation to one that is directly attentive to the "earthly" conditions with which human societies are inextricably linked. It is here, he suggests, that "a shift to the register of obligation invites a broader inquiry into our contemporary 'earthbound' condition at the level of the existential, pre-institutional and pre-contractual" (ibid., p. 689). Referring also to Simone Weil's notion of "rootedness" (*enracinement*) it identifies "the bonds that emerge out of the primary situatedness of human life and the web of relations through which the conditions of habitability can be maintained that are arguably lost with the emergence of a juridical rights discourse" (ibid., p. 688).

Reflecting back on the transformations identified earlier in this book with respect to the place and priority of obligations, this might suggest that a further "structural substitution" is now required, one that would relocate that sensibility to the "earth-bound" to a position of primacy. In this form, new "necessary obligations" (to draw on Godelier's observations in Chapter 1) would require instantiation as stationary points in ways that would have priority ahead of all further actions. In terms we drew from Stair, these obligations would be understood and acted on *as* necessary, as non-negotiable, as a new axiomatic form of obediential obligations with respect to the fragile and essential earth on which we depend.

For need too describes our relationship to the environment. Humans, as with other animal and plant species, are entirely dependent on the complex constitution and ongoing sustenance of the natural world. In this sense we are indeed all "supplicants", and the "illusion of self-sufficiency" engenders in this instance nothing short of the risk of collective suicide. If human activity has caused the problem, then the obligations to stop causing harms and to begin to mend so far as possible the fragile structures that support life seem fundamental. In this sense, the "ecology of obligation" is no longer merely a metaphor. It would describe the reality of our mutual relationships and joint liabilities within the complex webs of life that sustain human life and which we destroy at our (and other species') peril. Law's coercive power, *its* capacity to bind, may still be necessary in seeking to secure these obligations. But its limitations, particularly with respect to its forms and operations, must be constantly reviewed in light of its actual results and its ability to deliver for human and non-human relationships of solidarity. For as Roger Cotterrell observes, while solidarity "has to be worked for, and the wise crafting of law is a very important means of doing so, [it is] not the only or perhaps the most fundamental one" (Cotterrell 2018, p. 221).

Solidarities have not yet been created sufficiently to address contemporary political, technological, and ecological predicaments. But urgent attention to new trajectories of collective thought and action needs to be given. If these are to be imagined, and made possible, then obligations may have a key role to play in constituting and sustaining them. For if human societies collectively fail to imagine and institute a set of non-negotiable, non-commodifiable binding obligations, then, as the contemporary course of history makes clear, human futures, along with the many other species being sacrificed along the way, will be hot, wet, and increasingly short. Given this, to return to and to replenish the priority of obligations may be a wise and timely proposition.

Bibliography

Agamben, G, 2011, *The Sacrament of Language*, Stanford, Stanford UP.
Althusser, L, 2014, *On the Reproduction of Capitalism*, London, Verso.
Amis, M, 1988, *Einstein's Monsters*, London, Penguin.
Arendt, H, 2003, "Collective Responsibility", in J Kohn ed, *Responsibility and Judgment*, New York, Schocken, pp. 147–158.
Atiyah, P, 1979, *The Rise and Fall of Freedom of Contract*, Oxford, Clarendon Press.
Atria, F, 2015, "Social Rights, Social Contract, Socialism" 24(4) *Social & Legal Studies*, 598–613.
Atria, F, and Salgado, C, 2019, "Social Rights", in Christodoulidis et al., eds, *Research Handbook on Critical Legal Theory*, Cheltenham, Edward Elgar, pp. 363–378.
Benveniste, E, 1973, *Indo-European Language and Society*, London, Faber & Faber.
Bevan, A, 1952, *In Place of Fear*, New York, Simon and Schuster.
Birks, P, 2000, "Introduction", in P Birks ed, *English Private Law*, Volume 1, Oxford, OUP, pp. xxv–li.
Birks, P, 2014, *The Roman Law of Obligations*, ed. E Descheemaeker, Oxford, OUP.
Blyth, M, 2013, *Austerity*, Oxford, OUP.
Cameron, E, 2016, "Fidelity and Betrayal under Law", 16(2) *Oxford University Commonwealth Law Journal*, 346–360.
Campbell, AH, 1954, *The Structure of Stair's Institutions*, Glasgow, Jackson.
Chang, W, 2016, *In Search of the Way*, Edinburgh, EUP.
Chen, A, 2004, *An Introduction to the Legal System of the People's Republic of China*, 3rd ed, Hong Kong, LexisNexis.
Christodoulidis, E, 2017, "Social Rights Constitutionalism: An Antagonistic Endorsement" 44(1) *Journal of Law and Society*, 123–149.
Christodoulidis, E, 2018, "Dogma, or the Deep Rootedness of Obligation", in Matthews and Veitch, 2018.
Cohen, MR, 1927, "Property and Sovereignty" 13 *Cornell Law Review*, 8–30.
Collins, H, et al., 2019, "Introduction", in H Collins et al., *Philosophical Foundations of Labour Law*, Oxford, OUP, pp. 1–30.

Constable, M, 2014, *Our Word Is Our Bond*, Stanford, Stanford Law Books.
Cotterrell, R, 2018, *Sociological Jurisprudence*, Abingdon, Routledge.
Cover, RM, 1987, "Obligation: A Jewish Jurisprudence of the Social Order" 5(1) *Journal of Law and Religion*, 65–74.
Cox, H, 2016, *The Market as God*, Cambridge, MA, Harvard UP.
Curry, P, 2011, *Ecological Ethics*, 2nd ed, Cambridge, Polity.
Davies, M, 2017, *Law Unlimited*, Abingdon, Routledge.
Delmas, C, 2016, "Political Resistance for Hedgehogs", in W Waluchow and S Sciaraffa eds, *The Legacy of Ronald Dworkin*, Oxford, OUP, pp. 25–48.
D'Entreves, AP, 1951, *Natural Law*, London, Hutchinson.
Donne, J, 1623, Sermon IX, "Preached on Candlemas Day", available at https://www.biblestudytools.com/classics/the-works-of-john-donne-vol-1/sermon-ix.html, accessed 2 June 2019; no pagination available.
Dukes, R, 2019, "The Economic Sociology of Labour Law" 46(3) *Journal of Law and Society* 396–422.
Durkheim, E, 2014, *The Division of Labor in Society*, New York, Free Press.
Featherstone, D, 2012, *Solidarity*, London, Zed Books.
Finnis, J, 1980, *Natural Law and Natural Rights*, Oxford, Clarendon.
Foucault, M, 1984, "The Juridical Apparatus", in W Connolly ed, *Legitimacy and the State*, Oxford, Blackwell, pp. 201–221.
Foucault, M, 1990, *The History of Sexuality*, Volume 1, London, Penguin.
Foucault, M, 1995, *Discipline and Punish*, New York, Vintage.
Foucault, M, 2014, *On the Government of the Living*, Basingstoke, Palgrave Macmillan.
Frankfurt, H, 2000, "Some Mysteries of Love", The Lindley Lecture, University of Kansas, available at https://kuscholarworks.ku.edu/bitstream/handle/1808/12414/somemysteriesoflove-2001.pdf?sequence=1, accessed 6 April 2019.
Fried, C, 2015, "A conscience in hell", *New Rambler Review*, available at https://newramblerreview.com/book-reviews/law/a-conscience-in-hell, accessed 21 April 2019
FT 2019, "Global debt surges to highest level in peacetime", *Financial Times*, available at https://www.ft.com/content/661f5c8a-dec9-11e9-9743-db5a370481bc, last accessed 17 November 2019.
Gallagher, J, 2013, "Hanging together: The case for union", https://notesfromnorthbritain.files.wordpress.com/2013/10/hanging-together.pdf (last accessed 1 May 2020)
Garland, D, 2016, *The Welfare State*, Oxford, OUP.
Glasman, M, 1996, *Unnecessary Suffering*, London, Verso.
Godelier, M, 2011, *The Metamorphoses of Kinship*, London, Verso.
Goffman, E, 1968, *Asylums*, Harmondsworth, Penguin.
Graeber, D, 2012, *Debt*, Brooklyn, Melville House.
Graeber, D, 2016, *The Utopia of Rules*, Brooklyn, Melville House.
Haakonssen, K, 1996, *Natural Law and Moral Philosophy*, Cambridge, CUP.
Habermas, J, 1987, *The Theory of Communicative Action*, Volume 2, Cambridge, Polity.

Bibliography 117

Hale, R, 1923, "Coercion and Distribution in a Supposedly Non-Coercive State," 38 *Political Science Quarterly*, 470–478.
Hart, HLA, 1961, *The Concept of Law*, Oxford, Clarendon.
Hart, HLA, 1982, "Legal Duty and Obligation", in HLA Hart, *Essays on Bentham*, Oxford, OUP, pp. 127–161.
Harvey, D, 2010, *A Companion to Marx's* Capital, London, Verso.
Harvey, D, 2018, "Universal Alienation", 16(2) *tripleC*, 424–439.
Hobbes, T, 1996, *Leviathan*, Cambridge, CUP.
Hogg, M, 2017, *Obligations: Law and Language*, Cambridge, CUP.
Hohfeld, WN, 1964, *Fundamental Legal Conceptions as Applied in Judicial Reasoning*, ed W. W. Cook, New Haven, Yale UP.
Honore, T, 1987, *Making Law Bind*, Oxford, Clarendon.
Hume, D, 1987, "Of the Origin of Government", in Eugene F Miller ed, *Essays Moral, Political, and Literary*, Indianapolis, Liberty Press, pp. 37–41.
Ignatieff, M, 1984, *The Needs of Strangers*, London, Chatto & Windus.
Ireland, P, 2011, "Law and the Neoliberal Vision", 62(1) *Northern Ireland Law Quarterly*, 1–32.
Jacques, M, 2012, *When China Rules the World*, London, Allen Lane.
James, 1994, King VI and I [James Stuart], *Political Writings*, ed J Sommerville, Cambridge, CUP.
Jefferson, T, 1776, "The Declaration of Independence" (various editions).
Judt, T, 2010, *Ill Fares the Land*, London, Allen Lane.
Kant, I, 1996, *The Metaphysics of Morals*, Cambridge, CUP.
Kay, J, 2015, *Other People's Money*, London, Profile Books.
Kerrigan, J, 2016, *Shakespeare's Binding Language*, Oxford, OUP.
Kerruish, V, and Hunt, A, 1992, "Dworkin's Dutiful Daughter", in A Hunt ed, *Reading Dworkin Critically*, New York, Berg, pp. 209–239.
Korsgaard, C, 2008, "Taking the Law into Our Own Hands", in C Korsgaard ed, *The Constitution of Agency*, Oxford, OUP, pp. 233–262.
Locke, J, 1988, *Two Treatises of Government*, Cambridge, CUP.
Lordon, F, 2014, *Willing Slaves of Capital*, London, Verso.
MacCormick, N, 1982a, "Law, Obligation, and Consent: Reflections on Stair and Locke", in N MacCormick, *Legal Right and Social Democracy*, Oxford, Clarendon, pp. 60–83.
MacCormick, N, 1982b, "Law and Economics: Adam Smith's analysis", in N MacCormick, *Legal Right and Social Democracy*, Oxford, Clarendon, pp. 103–125.
MacCormick, N, 1990, "General Legal Concepts", in R Black et al. eds, *The Laws of Scotland: Stair Memorial Encyclopaedia, Vol 11*, Edinburgh, Butterworths, pp. 359–419.
MacCormick, N, 2007, *Institutions of Law*, Oxford, OUP.
MacCormick, N, 2008, *Practical Reason in Law and Morality*, Oxford, OUP.
MacIntyre, A, 1985, *After Virtue*, London, Duckworth.
MacIntyre, A, 1988, *Whose Justice? Which Rationality?*, London, Duckworth.
MacIntyre, A, 1999, *Dependent Rational Animals*, London, Duckworth.
MacIntyre, A, 2016, *Ethics in the Conflicts of Modernity*, Cambridge, CUP.

Manjapra, K, 2018, "When will Britain face up to its crimes against humanity?", available at https://www.theguardian.com/news/2018/mar/29/slavery-abolition-compensation-when-will-britain-face-up-to-its-crimes-against-humanity, last accessed 18 June 2019.
Mantena, K, 2010, *Alibis of Empire*, Princeton NJ, Princeton UP.
Marx, K, 1976, *Capital*, Volume 1, Harmondsworth, Penguin.
Matthews, D, 2019, "From Global to Anthropocenic Assemblages" 82(4) *Modern Law Review*, 665–691.
Matthews, D, and Veitch, S, eds, 2018, *Law, Obligation, Community*, Abingdon, Routledge.
McAlpine, R, 2014, *CommonWeal*, Glasgow, Scottish Left Review Press.
McGee, K, 2014, *Bruno Latour: The Normativity of Networks*, Abingdon, Routledge.
McIlvanney, W, 1991, *Surviving the Shipwreck*, Edinburgh, Mainstream.
Mckinsey 2015, "Debt and (not much) deleveraging", available at http://www.mckinsey.com/global-themes/employment-and-growth/debt-and-not-much-deleveraging, last accessed 17 November 2019.
Mckinsey 2018, "A decade after the financial crisis, what has (and hasn't) changed", available at https://www.mckinsey.com/, last accessed 17 November 2019.
Milgram, S, 1974, *Obedience to Authority*, New York, Harper.
Milgram, S, 1992, *The Individual in a Social World*, New York, McGraw-Hill.
Miller, WG, 1903, *The Data of Jurisprudence*, Edinburgh, W Green.
Mills, CW, 1956, *The Power Elite*, New York, OUP.
Moyn, S, 2010, *The Last Utopia*, Cambridge, MA, Belknap Press.
Moyn, S, 2017, "Reclaiming the history of duties", in S Moyn ed, *Human Rights and the Uses of History*, London, Verso, pp. 151–168.
Nietzsche, F, 1996, *On The Genealogy of Morals*, Oxford, OUP.
O'Neill, O, 2000, "Women's Rights: Whose Obligations?", in O O'Neill ed, *Bounds of Justice* Cambridge, CUP, pp. 97–112.
Oxfam, 2019, "Billionaire fortunes grew by $2.5 billion a day last year as poorest saw their wealth fall", available at https://www.oxfam.org/en/press-releases/billionaire-fortunes-grew-25-billion-day-last-year-poorest-saw-their-wealth-fall, last accessed 21 October 2020.
Pashukanis, EB, 2002, *The General Theory of Law and Marxism*, New Brunswick, Transaction Publishers.
Pensky, M, 2008, *The Ends of Solidarity*, Albany, SUNY Press.
Pistor, K, 2019, *The Code of Capital*, Princeton, Princeton UP.
Polanyi, K, 1957, *The Great Transformation*, New York, Beacon Press.
Raz, J, 1986, *The Morality of Freedom*, Oxford, Clarendon Press.
Reuters 2017, "Total global debt tops 325 per cent of GDP as government debt jumps", available at http://www.reuters.com/article/us-global-debt-iif-idUSKBN14O1PQ, last accessed 17 November 2019.
Reuters 2019, "China's debt now tops 300% of GDP, now 15% of global total", https://www.reuters.com/article/us-china-economy-debt/chinas-debt-

tops-300-of-gdp-now-15-of-global-total-iif-idUSKCN1UD0KD, last accessed 21 November 2019.
Rogan, T, 2017, *The Moral Economists*, Princeton, Princeton UP.
Rousseau, J-J, 1973, *The Social Contract and Discourses*, London, Dent.
Schell, J, 1982, *The Fate of the Earth*, London, Jonathan Cape.
Shaw, Lord, 1923, "Law as a Link of Empire" 1 *Canadian Bar Review* 19.
Shrubsole, G, 2019, *Who Owns England?*, London, Collins.
Simmel, G, 1964, *The Sociology of Georg Simmel*, Glencoe, IL, The Free Press.
Smith, A, 1976, *The Wealth of Nations*, Oxford, OUP.
Smith, A, 1978, *Lectures on Jurisprudence*, RL Meek et al. eds, Oxford, OUP.
Sommerville, J, 1994, "Introduction" to James 1994, pp. xv–xxviii.
Stair, Viscount, 1981, (James Dalrymple), *Institutions of the Law of Scotland*, Edinburgh and Glasgow, University Presses.
Streeck, W, 2014, *Buying Time*, London, Verso.
Supiot, A, 2007, *Homo Juridicus*, London, Verso.
Supiot, A, 2018, *Governance by Numbers*, London, Bloomsbury.
Tawney, RM, 1964, *Equality*, 4th ed., London, Unwin.
Thompson, EP, 1971, "The Moral Economy of the English Crowd in the Eighteenth Century", 50 *Past and Present*, 76–136.
Thompson, EP, 1993, "Time, Work-Discipline, and Industrial Capitalism", in EP Thompson, *Customs in Common*, London, Penguin, pp. 352–402.
Tierney, B, 2001, *The Idea of Natural Rights*, Michigan, Eerdmans.
TJN 2019, Tax Justice Network (various updated reports), https://www.taxjustice.net (last accessed 17 October 2019).
Tolhurst, G, 2006, *The Assignment of Contractual Rights*, Oxford, Hart.
Tuck, 1978, *Natural Rights Theories*, Cambridge, CUP.
UN 2019, "Scourge of slavery still claims 40 million victims worldwide", available at https://news.un.org/en/story/2019/09/1045972, last accessed 11 November 2019.
Usher, RG, 1903, "James I and Sir Edward Coke", 18 *English Historical Review*, 664–675.
Veitch, S, 2007, *Law and Irresponsibility: On the Legitimation of Human Suffering*, Abingdon, Routledge.
Veitch, S, 2018, "Duty Free", in Matthews and Veitch 2018, pp. 101–121.
Waldron, J, 1989, "Rights in Conflict" 99 *Ethics*, 503–519.
Waldron, J, 2000, "The Role of Rights in Practical Reasoning: 'Rights' versus 'Needs'", 4 *The Journal of Ethics*, 115–135.
Watson, I, 2014, *Aboriginal Peoples, Colonialism and International Law*, Abingdon, Routledge.
Weber, M, 1930, *The Protestant Ethic and the Spirit of Capitalism*, London, Allen & Unwin.
Weil, S, 2005, *Simone Weil: An Anthology*, Harmondsworth, Penguin.
Williams, B, 1994, *Shame and Necessity*, Berkeley, University of California Press.

Williams, R, 1988, *Keywords*, London, Fontana Press.

Williams Jr, R A, 1987, "Taking Rights Aggressively: the Perils and Promise of Critical Legal Theory for Peoples of Color" 5(1) *Law & Inequality: A Journal of Theory and Practice*, 103–134.

Zimmermann, R, 1996, *The Law of Obligations*, Oxford, OUP.

Index

Aboriginal peoples 9
Aeschylus 61
Anthropocene 112
apartheid 47
Aquinas, T 22, 38
Arendt, H 34, 36
Aristotle 22, 36
Atiyah, P 74
Atria, F 95

Baxter, R 51
being obliged 28
Bentham, J 59
Benveniste, E 104
Bevan, A 48
binding quality of obligations 1, 5, 8, 11, 13–14, 25, 27, 30, 58ff., 104, 111, 113
Birks, P 4, 59–60, 62, 89
Buchanan, G 24, 26

Cameron, E 47–8, 97
Campbell, AH 60
capitalism 49–53, 77–81, 111
Charles I 24
Christianity 10, 20, 22, 30, 33, 51
Christodoulidis, E 104
citizenship, active and passive 41–3, 47
coercive laws of competition 51
Cohen, M 80
Coke, E 25–7
collateralized debt obligation 66
collective action 109

collective autonomy 39
collective obligations 97, 101
collective well-being 90ff.
Collins, H 74
colonialism 44–6, 49
commodification 65, 67, 76, 78–9, 108, 111
commodification of labour 53, 55, 73, 79
common good 103–7, 109
compulsion in law 60–2
Confucianism 9
constitutional law 52, 79, 86
constitutive obligations 25, 27, 70
contract for work 53, 73ff.
correlation between legal rights and obligations 1, 87, 90–1, 93, 95, 101
correlation been needs and obligations 91, 98, 101
Cotterrell, R 113
Cover, R 9
Cox, H 50
creditors' rights 87–8

debt 28ff., 65–6, 85ff., 102
decommodification 108
Delmas, C 109
dependency 98, 102, 104, 106–7, 111, 113
dignity 91, 98, 100, 104, 107, 109, 111
distrust 108
divine right of kings 23–7
Donne, J 27ff., 51, 55

ecology of obligations 67ff.
environment 92–3, 110–3
exploitation 19, 51, 56, 104, 108–9, 111

family 14–15, 17, 83, 92
financial property 81
Finnis, J 22
Foucault, M 27, 57, 70
Frankfurt, H 14–15
free labour 52–5
free riders 82
Fried, C 4
friendship 14–15, 17

Gaius 4
Gallagher, J 105
Garland, D 97
general will 40
gift 16
Glasman, M 106
Godelier, M 15–17, 112
Goffman, E 63
governance by numbers 75
Graeber, D 30, 52, 65
Greenspan, A 89
Grotius, H 22, 33

Haakonssen, K 22–3
Habermas, J 13
Hale, R 79–80
Hart, HLA 5, 45–6, 59
Harvey, D 51, 86
Hobbes, T 38, 71, 83
Hohfeld, WN 93
Honore, T 18–19
human resources 75
human rights 1, 22, 85
Hume, D 38–9
hybrids of obligation and obedience 6, 58, 67ff., 73ff.

Ignatieff, M 99
indebtedness 1, 31, 65, 85ff.
indigenous peoples 44–5
indignity 47, 109
inequality 3, 42–3, 47, 58, 65, 87, 108, 110
Ireland, P 81

James, VI & I 23ff., 37
Jefferson, T 15, 39, 107–8
joint liability 102–9, 113
Judaism 9, 20
Judt, T 66
Justinian 4, 10, 59

Kant, I 38ff., 62, 89
Kay, J 66
Kerrigan, J 14
Korsgaard, C 40

law of value 78–80, 82–4, 88
language use 11–14
league tables 76
legal bond 58ff.
legal coercion 67, 79–80
legal persons 62ff., 78
legal positivism 45–6
Locke, J 24, 26, 35, 38
Lordon, F 49
love 14–15, 90, 100, 102

MacCormick, N 11–12, 35, 61, 63, 81
McGee, K 68
McIllvanney, W 99
MacIntyre, A 10, 34, 48, 99, 101
Macleod, HD 65
Maine, H 54
management by objectives 75
Mantena, K 44
market forces 80, 84, 88–9
Marx, K 49–50
Matthews, D 112
Milgram, S 17, 83
Miller, WG 17–18, 34
Mills, CW 107
mindfulness 77
moral economy 56
Moyn, S 35, 52, 85

national borders 108–9
natural law 22, 24, 29, 32–3, 36
natural right 23, 36
necessary obligations 16–17, 93, 112
necessity 49–50, 60–2, 78, 83–4

needs 91, 98ff., 113
Nietzsche, F 17–18
normative aspect of obligations 61–2, 69

oaths 13–14, 25, 31
obediential obligations 32–4, 50, 69, 79
obligation and identity 63–4, 104
obligation to resist 109
Ogden Tables 111
O'Neill, O 95ff.

Pashukanis, EB 78, 80
performance indicators 75
Polanyi, K 53–4, 106
practices of obedience 2–3, 6, 9, 22, 37, 49, 69–72, 83–6
primordial debt 28–9, 88
property rights 2–3, 33, 48, 52–3, 79–81, 110–1
Pufendorf, S 14

Reid, D 34
reliance 14, 68, 98–9
right to education 94, 96
Rogan, T 110
role obligation 63–5
Roman Law 10–11, 17–18, 22, 59, 65, 102
Rousseau, J-J 38–40, 83

sanction 61–2, 67
Schell, J 110
Shaw, Lord 44
Simmel, G 42, 53
slavery 43, 47, 63, 86
slow pedagogy 95
Smith, A 53–4, 77–8, 82

social and economic rights 94–7
social bond 103–4
social contract 33, 35, 38ff.
socialism 55
solidarity 56, 90–2, 102ff.
sovereign right 52, 110
sovereignty 9, 39, 80, 86, 110
Stair, Viscount 29, 31ff., 50, 79
Streeck, W 85–7
structural substitution 6, 43, 48, 49, 112
Suarez, F 22
Supiot, A 11, 75

Tawney, RM 3
tax evasion 82, 105–6
taxation 3, 82, 105–6
Taylor, C 95
Thompson, EP 56
time-keeping 84
trust 13–14, 68, 90, 104, 108
Tuck, R 10

uncalculated giving and receiving 99, 110

Villey, M 22
vinculum iuris 59, 61, 66, 71, 89, 97
vulnerability 87–8, 92, 98–9, 102–4, 111

Waldron, J 93, 101–2
waves of duties 93–4, 97, 101–109
Weber, M 51–2
Weil, S 91, 98–9, 112
welfare state 82, 99–100
Williams, B 61

Zimmermann, R 18, 60, 62

For Product Safety Concerns and Information please contact our EU representative GPSR@taylorandfrancis.com
Taylor & Francis Verlag GmbH, Kaufingerstraße 24, 80331 München, Germany

www.ingramcontent.com/pod-product-compliance
Lightning Source LLC
Chambersburg PA
CBHW051753230426
43670CB00012B/2269